The Homemade Pizza Cookbook:

Unlock the Secrets to Authentic Pizza with 150 Delectable Recipes from Italy to New York and Chicago

Copyright © 2023 by Mario Napolitani. All rights reserved.

This cookbook and the content provided herein, including but not limited to, text, design, graphics, images, and recipes, are the exclusive property of Mario Napolitani and are protected under international copyright laws.

No part of this cookbook may be reproduced, distributed, or transmitted in any form or by any means, including photocopying, recording, or other electronic or mechanical methods, without the prior written permission of the publisher, except in the case of brief quotations embodied in critical reviews and certain other noncommercial uses permitted by copyright law.

Disclaimer

While every effort has been made to ensure the accuracy of the information in this cookbook, the author and publisher accept no responsibility for errors or omissions, or for any consequences arising from the use of the information contained herein.

This cookbook is intended to provide general information on the topics presented and is not an exhaustive treatment of such subjects. All recipes are intended to be prepared by adults or with adult supervision and the author and publisher are not responsible for any injuries or damages that may result.

The reader assumes all risks associated with the preparation and consumption of the dishes detailed in this cookbook. Always consult a medical professional before making significant changes to your diet.

Table of Contents

Classic Margherita Pizza 8

Pepperoni Perfection Pizza 8

Hearty Meat Lover's Pizza 9

Four-Cheese Gourmet Pizza 9

Spicy Buffalo Chicken Pizza 10

Artisan Veggie Delight Pizza 10

Tuscan Truffle Pizza 11

Smoked Salmon and Cream Cheese Pizza 11

Sweet Pineapple and Ham Hawaiian Pizza 12

Capricciosa Italian Style Pizza 12

Mediterranean Greek Pizza 13

BBQ Chicken Feast Pizza 13

Spanish Chorizo and Olive Pizza 14

Seafood Extravaganza Pizza 14

Italian Prosciutto and Arugula Pizza 15

Creamy Garlic Chicken Pizza 15

Spicy Sausage and Pepper Pizza 16

Pesto and Sun-Dried Tomato Pizza 16

Shrimp Scampi Pizza 17

French Onion Style Pizza 17

Philly Cheesesteak Pizza 18

Eggplant Parmesan Pizza 18

Fig, Prosciutto, and Blue Cheese Pizza 19

Sweet & Spicy Korean BBQ Pizza 19

Balsamic Glazed Caprese Pizza 20

Lobster and Sweet Corn Pizza 20

Spinach and Feta Stuffed Crust Pizza 21

Bacon and Egg Breakfast Pizza 21

Black and White Truffle Pizza 22

Taco Fiesta Pizza 22

French Ratatouille Pizza 23

Sweet and Savory Apple Gorgonzola Pizza 23

Rustic Butternut Squash and Sage Pizza 24

Cajun Shrimp and Andouille Pizza 24

Spicy Jerk Chicken Pizza	25
Chocolate and Marshmallow Dessert Pizza	25
Middle Eastern Lamb and Feta Pizza	26
Smoky Pulled Pork Pizza	26
Chicken Tikka Masala Pizza	27
Quattro Formaggi (Four Cheese) Pizza	27
Spicy Italian Sausage Pizza	28
Caramelized Onion and Goat Cheese Pizza	28
Wild Mushroom and Thyme Pizza	29
Pear and Gorgonzola Pizza	29
Clam and Garlic Pizza	30
Chili Cheese Dog Pizza	30
Provolone and Roasted Pepper Pizza	31
Buffalo Mozzarella and Basil Pizza	31
Sweet Potato and Kale Pizza	32
Roasted Garlic and White Sauce Pizza	32
Black Olive and Feta Cheese Pizza	33
BBQ Pulled Pork Pizza	33
Fresh Tomato and Basil Pizza	34
Roasted Brussels Sprouts and Bacon Pizza	34
Spicy Tandoori Chicken Pizza	35
Bacon Cheeseburger Pizza	35
French Fry and Gravy Pizza	36
Chipotle Chicken Pizza	36
Prosciutto and Fig Pizza	37
Sausage and Rapini Pizza	37
Caramelized Pear and Blue Cheese Pizza	38
Zucchini and Herbed Ricotta Pizza	38
Pumpkin and Sage Pizza	39
Italian Salami and Red Onion Pizza	39
Chicken Alfredo Pizza	40
Recipe's Name: Anchovy and Capers Pizza	40
Asparagus and Hollandaise Pizza	41
Buffalo Cauliflower Pizza	41
Bacon Jalapeno Popper Pizza	42

Crab Rangoon Pizza 42

Grilled Chicken and Pesto Pizza 43

Shaved Asparagus and Parmesan Pizza 43

Cherry Tomato and Mozzarella Pizza 44

Brie and Cranberry Pizza 44

Beer Cheese and Bratwurst Pizza 45

Sesame Chicken Pizza 45

Creamy Leek and Pancetta Pizza 46

Kalamata Olive and Greek Feta Pizza 46

Italian Meatball and Ricotta Pizza 47

Pecan, Pear, and Gorgonzola Pizza 47

Spaghetti and Meatball Pizza 48

Chicken, Spinach, and Artichoke Pizza 48

Italian Sausage and Roasted Red Pepper Pizza 49

Broccoli and Cheddar Pizza 49

Garlic Prawn and Fresh Chili Pizza 50

Squid Ink and Seafood Pizza 50

Turkey and Cranberry Thanksgiving Pizza 51

Roasted Potato and Rosemary Pizza 51

Chorizo and Manchego Pizza 52

Brisket and Pickles Pizza 52

Mexican Street Corn Pizza 53

Lebanese Lamb and Pomegranate Pizza 53

Provolone, Mushroom, and Truffle Oil Pizza 54

Chicken, Brie, and Apple Pizza 54

Bacon, Lettuce, and Tomato Pizza 55

Reuben Sandwich Pizza 55

Cordon Bleu Pizza 56

Vietnamese Banh Mi Pizza 56

English Breakfast Pizza 57

Chicken Souvlaki Pizza 57

Sausage and Gravy Breakfast Pizza 58

Goat Cheese and Red Beet Pizza 58

Sausage, Peppers, and Onions Pizza 59

Chimichurri Steak Pizza 59

Peking Duck Pizza	60
Apple, Walnut, and Blue Cheese Pizza	60
Lemon, Smoked Salmon, and Dill Pizza	61
Barbecue Jackfruit Pizza	61
Blue Cheese and Hot Honey Pizza	62
Pastrami and Pickles Pizza	62
Shrimp and Grits Pizza	63
Pulled Pork and Coleslaw Pizza	63
Curry Chicken Pizza	64
Chicken, Bacon, Ranch Pizza	64
Garlic, Spinach, and Chicken Pizza	65
Hawaiian BBQ Chicken Pizza	65
Tomato, Basil, and Mozzarella Pizza	66
Philly Cheesesteak Pizza	66
Baked Ziti Pizza	67
Guacamole and Shrimp Pizza	67
Taco Supreme Pizza	68
Chicken Quesadilla Pizza	68
Pad Thai Pizza	69
Pulled Pork and Pineapple Pizza	69
Fennel Sausage and Pepper Pizza	70
Teriyaki Chicken and Pineapple Pizza	70
Margherita with Balsamic Reduction Pizza	71
Shrimp, Lobster, and Crab Pizza	71
Portobello and Spinach Pizza	72
Chicken Parmesan Pizza	72
Provolone and Pepperoni Pizza	73
Pesto, Mozzarella, and Tomato Pizza	73
Alfredo, Chicken, and Broccoli Pizza	74
Ricotta, Mozzarella, and Basil Pizza	74
Goat Cheese and Spinach Pizza	75
Egg, Bacon, and Spinach Breakfast Pizza	75
Pancetta, Arugula, and Tomato Pizza	76
Eggplant, Tomato, and Pesto Pizza	76
Butternut Squash and Caramelized Onion Pizza	77

Vegan Margherita Pizza 77

Gluten-Free Pepperoni Pizza 78

Vegetarian Supreme Pizza 78

Vegan BBQ Jackfruit Pizza 79

Gluten-Free Veggie Pizza 79

Keto Chicken and Spinach Pizza 80

Vegan Roasted Vegetable Pizza 80

Keto Meat Lover's Pizza 81

Vegan Mushroom and Bell Pepper Pizza 81

Gluten-Free Hawaiian Pizza 82

Keto Pepperoni and Cheese Pizza 82

Classic Margherita Pizza

Yield: 4 servings | Prep Time: 20 minutes | Cook Time: 15 minutes

Ingredients:

- Pizza dough
- Tomato sauce
- Fresh basil leaves
- Fresh mozzarella
- Olive oil

Directions:

1. Preheat your oven to 475°F (245°C).
2. Roll out the pizza dough to your preferred thickness.
3. Spread a thin layer of tomato sauce over the dough.
4. Arrange slices of mozzarella cheese and basil leaves on top.
5. Drizzle a bit of olive oil over the pizza.
6. Bake for 15 minutes or until cheese is bubbling and slightly golden.

Nutritional Information: 425 calories, 20g protein, 55g carbohydrates, 15g fat, 2g fiber, 45mg cholesterol, 980mg sodium, 250mg potassium.

Pepperoni Perfection Pizza

Yield: 4 servings | Prep Time: 20 minutes | Cook Time: 15 minutes

Ingredients:

- Pizza dough
- Tomato sauce
- Pepperoni slices
- Mozzarella cheese

Directions:

1. Preheat your oven to 475°F (245°C).
2. Roll out your pizza dough to your preferred thickness.
3. Spread a thin layer of tomato sauce over the dough.
4. Arrange pepperoni slices and cover with mozzarella cheese.
5. Bake for 15 minutes or until cheese is bubbling and slightly golden.

Nutritional Information: 530 calories, 25g protein, 55g carbohydrates, 25g fat, 2g fiber, 70mg cholesterol, 1,280mg sodium, 300mg potassium.

Hearty Meat Lover's Pizza

Yield: 4 servings | Prep Time: 20 minutes | Cook Time: 15 minutes

Ingredients:

- Pizza dough
- Tomato sauce
- Pepperoni slices
- Ground sausage
- Diced ham
- Mozzarella cheese

Directions:

1. Preheat your oven to 475°F (245°C).
2. Roll out your pizza dough to your preferred thickness.
3. Spread a thin layer of tomato sauce over the dough.
4. Evenly distribute the pepperoni, sausage, and ham.
5. Cover with mozzarella cheese.
6. Bake for 15 minutes or until cheese is bubbly and slightly golden.

Nutritional Information: 610 calories, 35g protein, 55g carbohydrates, 30g fat, 2g fiber, 90mg cholesterol, 1,630mg sodium, 350mg potassium.

Four-Cheese Gourmet Pizza

Yield: 4 servings | Prep Time: 20 minutes | Cook Time: 15 minutes

Ingredients:

- Pizza dough
- Tomato sauce
- Mozzarella cheese
- Cheddar cheese
- Parmesan cheese
- Blue cheese

Directions:

1. Preheat your oven to 475°F (245°C).
2. Roll out your pizza dough to your preferred thickness.
3. Spread a thin layer of tomato sauce over the dough.
4. Sprinkle the four cheeses evenly over the sauce.
5. Bake for 15 minutes or until cheese is bubbly and slightly golden.

Nutritional Information: 590 calories, 30g protein, 55g carbohydrates, 30g fat, 2g fiber, 80mg cholesterol, 1,320mg sodium, 300mg potassium.

Spicy Buffalo Chicken Pizza

Yield: 4 servings | Prep Time: 20 minutes | Cook Time: 15 minutes

Ingredients:

- Pizza dough
- Buffalo sauce
- Cooked chicken, shredded
- Mozzarella cheese
- Blue cheese crumbles
- Celery, thinly sliced

Directions:

1. Preheat your oven to 475°F (245°C).
2. Roll out your pizza dough to your preferred thickness.
3. Spread a layer of Buffalo sauce over the dough.
4. Distribute the shredded chicken and mozzarella over the sauce.
5. Sprinkle blue cheese and celery on top.
6. Bake for 15 minutes or until cheese is bubbly and slightly golden.

Nutritional Information: 600 calories, 35g protein, 55g carbohydrates, 28g fat, 2g fiber, 85mg cholesterol, 1,590mg sodium, 350mg potassium.

Artisan Veggie Delight Pizza

Yield: 4 servings | Prep Time: 20 minutes | Cook Time: 15 minutes

Ingredients:

- Pizza dough
- Tomato sauce
- Bell peppers
- Red onion
- Mushrooms
- Black olives
- Mozzarella cheese

Directions:

1. Preheat your oven to 475°F (245°C).
2. Roll out your pizza dough to your preferred thickness.
3. Spread a thin layer of tomato sauce over the dough.
4. Evenly distribute the bell peppers, red onion, mushrooms, and black olives.
5. Top with mozzarella cheese.
6. Bake for 15 minutes or until cheese is bubbling and slightly golden.

Nutritional Information: 400 calories, 20g protein, 58g carbohydrates, 12g fat, 5g fiber, 30mg cholesterol, 960mg sodium, 400mg potassium.

Tuscan Truffle Pizza

Yield: 4 servings | Prep Time: 20 minutes | Cook Time: 15 minutes

Ingredients:

- Pizza dough
- Olive oil
- Garlic, minced
- Mozzarella cheese
- Mushrooms
- Truffle oil

Directions:

1. Preheat your oven to 475°F (245°C).
2. Roll out your pizza dough to your preferred thickness.
3. Mix olive oil with minced garlic and spread over the dough.
4. Distribute mushrooms and top with mozzarella cheese.
5. Bake for 15 minutes or until cheese is bubbling and slightly golden.
6. Drizzle with truffle oil just before serving.

Nutritional Information: 410 calories, 18g protein, 45g carbohydrates, 18g fat, 2g fiber, 30mg cholesterol, 650mg sodium, 200mg potassium.

Smoked Salmon and Cream Cheese Pizza

Yield: 4 servings | Prep Time: 20 minutes | Cook Time: 15 minutes

Ingredients:

- Pizza dough
- Cream cheese
- Smoked salmon
- Red onion, thinly sliced
- Capers

Directions:

1. Preheat your oven to 475°F (245°C).
2. Roll out your pizza dough to your preferred thickness.
3. Spread a layer of cream cheese over the dough.
4. Arrange the smoked salmon, red onion slices, and capers.
5. Bake for 15 minutes or until edges are slightly golden.

Nutritional Information: 420 calories, 25g protein, 45g carbohydrates, 15g fat, 2g fiber, 35mg cholesterol, 950mg sodium, 200mg potassium.

Sweet Pineapple and Ham Hawaiian Pizza

Yield: 4 servings | Prep Time: 20 minutes | Cook Time: 15 minutes

Ingredients:

- Pizza dough
- Tomato sauce
- Ham, diced
- Pineapple chunks
- Mozzarella cheese

Directions:

1. Preheat your oven to 475°F (245°C).
2. Roll out your pizza dough to your preferred thickness.
3. Spread a thin layer of tomato sauce over the dough.
4. Distribute the diced ham and pineapple chunks.
5. Top with mozzarella cheese.
6. Bake for 15 minutes or until cheese is bubbling and slightly golden.

Nutritional Information: 410 calories, 20g protein, 50g carbohydrates, 15g fat, 2g fiber, 40mg cholesterol, 1,020mg sodium, 200mg potassium.

Capricciosa Italian Style Pizza

Yield: 4 servings | Prep Time: 20 minutes | Cook Time: 15 minutes

Ingredients:

- Pizza dough
- Tomato sauce
- Mozzarella cheese
- Ham, diced
- Mushrooms
- Artichoke hearts
- Black olives

Directions:

1. Preheat your oven to 475°F (245°C).
2. Roll out your pizza dough to your preferred thickness.
3. Spread a thin layer of tomato sauce over the dough.
4. Arrange the diced ham, mushrooms, artichoke hearts, and black olives.
5. Cover with mozzarella cheese.
6. Bake for 15 minutes or until cheese is bubbly and slightly golden.

Nutritional Information: 400 calories, 20g protein, 50g carbohydrates, 15g fat, 5g fiber, 40mg cholesterol, 1,100mg sodium, 300mg potassium.

Mediterranean Greek Pizza

Yield: 4 servings | Prep Time: 20 minutes | Cook Time: 15 minutes

Ingredients:

- Pizza dough
- Olive oil
- Garlic, minced
- Feta cheese
- Olives
- Tomatoes
- Red onion
- Spinach

Directions:

1. Preheat your oven to 475°F (245°C).
2. Roll out your pizza dough to your preferred thickness.
3. Mix olive oil with minced garlic and spread over the dough.
4. Distribute feta cheese, olives, tomatoes, red onion, and spinach evenly.
5. Bake for 15 minutes or until edges are slightly golden.

Nutritional Information: 380 calories, 15g protein, 50g carbohydrates, 15g fat, 3g fiber, 20mg cholesterol, 890mg sodium, 290mg potassium.

BBQ Chicken Feast Pizza

Yield: 4 servings | Prep Time: 20 minutes | Cook Time: 20 minutes

Ingredients:

- Pizza dough
- BBQ sauce
- Cooked chicken, shredded
- Red onion, thinly sliced
- Mozzarella cheese
- Cilantro leaves

Directions:

1. Preheat your oven to 475°F (245°C).
2. Roll out your pizza dough to your preferred thickness.
3. Spread a layer of BBQ sauce over the dough.
4. Arrange the shredded chicken, red onion slices.
5. Top with mozzarella cheese.
6. Bake for 20 minutes or until cheese is bubbling and slightly golden.
7. Garnish with cilantro leaves just before serving.

Nutritional Information: 450 calories, 25g protein, 52g carbohydrates, 16g fat, 2g fiber, 50mg cholesterol, 1,080mg sodium, 280mg potassium.

Spanish Chorizo and Olive Pizza

Yield: 4 servings | Prep Time: 20 minutes | Cook Time: 15 minutes

Ingredients:

- Pizza dough
- Tomato sauce
- Spanish chorizo, thinly sliced
- Olives
- Mozzarella cheese

Directions:

1. Preheat your oven to 475°F (245°C).
2. Roll out your pizza dough to your preferred thickness.
3. Spread a thin layer of tomato sauce over the dough.
4. Distribute the chorizo slices and olives.
5. Top with mozzarella cheese.
6. Bake for 15 minutes or until cheese is bubbling and slightly golden.

Nutritional Information: 420 calories, 22g protein, 50g carbohydrates, 18g fat, 3g fiber, 45mg cholesterol, 1,160mg sodium, 270mg potassium.

Seafood Extravaganza Pizza

Yield: 4 servings | Prep Time: 30 minutes | Cook Time: 20 minutes

Ingredients:

- Pizza dough
- Tomato sauce
- Shrimps, peeled
- Clams
- Squid, sliced
- Mozzarella cheese
- Parsley, chopped

Directions:

1. Preheat your oven to 475°F (245°C).
2. Roll out your pizza dough to your preferred thickness.
3. Spread a thin layer of tomato sauce over the dough.
4. Arrange the shrimps, clams, and squid slices.
5. Cover with mozzarella cheese.
6. Bake for 20 minutes or until seafood is cooked and cheese is bubbly.
7. Garnish with chopped parsley just before serving.

Nutritional Information: 450 calories, 30g protein, 52g carbohydrates, 12g fat, 2g fiber, 130mg cholesterol, 1,210mg sodium, 370mg potassium.

Italian Prosciutto and Arugula Pizza

Yield: 4 servings | Prep Time: 20 minutes | Cook Time: 15 minutes

Ingredients:

- Pizza dough
- Olive oil
- Garlic, minced
- Mozzarella cheese
- Prosciutto, thinly sliced
- Arugula

Directions:

1. Preheat your oven to 475°F (245°C).
2. Roll out your pizza dough to your preferred thickness.
3. Mix olive oil with minced garlic and spread over the dough.
4. Top with mozzarella cheese and prosciutto slices.
5. Bake for 15 minutes or until cheese is bubbling and slightly golden.
6. Garnish with arugula just before serving.

Nutritional Information: 410 calories, 20g protein, 45g carbohydrates, 18g fat, 3g fiber, 45mg cholesterol, 1,000mg sodium, 200mg potassium.

Creamy Garlic Chicken Pizza

Yield: 4 servings | Prep Time: 20 minutes | Cook Time: 20 minutes

Ingredients:

- Pizza dough
- Garlic cream sauce
- Cooked chicken, shredded
- Mozzarella cheese
- Parsley, chopped

Directions:

1. Preheat your oven to 475°F (245°C).
2. Roll out your pizza dough to your preferred thickness.
3. Spread garlic cream sauce over the dough.
4. Arrange the shredded chicken and cover with mozzarella cheese.
5. Bake for 20 minutes or until cheese is bubbling and slightly golden.
6. Garnish with chopped parsley just before serving.

Nutritional Information: 410 calories, 22g protein, 48g carbohydrates, 16g fat, 2g fiber, 45mg cholesterol, 960mg sodium, 250mg potassium.

Spicy Sausage and Pepper Pizza

Yield: 4 servings | Prep Time: 20 minutes | Cook Time: 20 minutes

Ingredients:

- Pizza dough
- Tomato sauce
- Spicy sausage, sliced
- Bell peppers, sliced
- Mozzarella cheese

Directions:

1. Preheat your oven to 475°F (245°C).
2. Roll out your pizza dough to your preferred thickness.
3. Spread a thin layer of tomato sauce over the dough.
4. Arrange the sausage slices and bell peppers.
5. Top with mozzarella cheese.
6. Bake for 20 minutes or until cheese is bubbling and slightly golden.

Nutritional Information: 480 calories, 24g protein, 50g carbohydrates, 22g fat, 3g fiber, 60mg cholesterol, 1,150mg sodium, 320mg potassium.

Pesto and Sun-Dried Tomato Pizza

Yield: 4 servings | Prep Time: 20 minutes | Cook Time: 15 minutes

Ingredients:

- Pizza dough
- Pesto sauce
- Sun-dried tomatoes
- Mozzarella cheese

Directions:

1. Preheat your oven to 475°F (245°C).
2. Roll out your pizza dough to your preferred thickness.
3. Spread pesto sauce over the dough.
4. Arrange the sun-dried tomatoes and cover with mozzarella cheese.
5. Bake for 15 minutes or until cheese is bubbling and slightly golden.

Nutritional Information: 400 calories, 18g protein, 48g carbohydrates, 18g fat, 3g fiber, 40mg cholesterol, 960mg sodium, 290mg potassium.

Shrimp Scampi Pizza

Yield: 4 servings | Prep Time: 30 minutes | Cook Time: 20 minutes

Ingredients:

- Pizza dough
- Garlic butter sauce
- Shrimps, peeled
- Mozzarella cheese
- Parsley, chopped

Directions:

1. Preheat your oven to 475°F (245°C).
2. Roll out your pizza dough to your preferred thickness.
3. Spread garlic butter sauce over the dough.
4. Arrange the shrimps and cover with mozzarella cheese.
5. Bake for 20 minutes or until shrimps are cooked and cheese is bubbly.
6. Garnish with chopped parsley just before serving.

Nutritional Information: 440 calories, 26g protein, 52g carbohydrates, 16g fat, 2g fiber, 120mg cholesterol, 1,090mg sodium, 300mg potassium.

French Onion Style Pizza

Yield: 4 servings | Prep Time: 30 minutes | Cook Time: 30 minutes

Ingredients:

- Pizza dough
- Caramelized onions
- Gruyere cheese
- Thyme leaves

Directions:

1. Preheat your oven to 475°F (245°C).
2. Roll out your pizza dough to your preferred thickness.
3. Spread caramelized onions over the dough.
4. Top with Gruyere cheese and thyme leaves.
5. Bake for 30 minutes or until cheese is bubbly and slightly golden.

Nutritional Information: 460 calories, 20g protein, 52g carbohydrates, 20g fat, 4g fiber, 60mg cholesterol, 1,080mg sodium, 320mg potassium.

Philly Cheesesteak Pizza

Yield: 4 servings | Prep Time: 20 minutes | Cook Time: 20 minutes

Ingredients:

- Pizza dough
- Thinly sliced beef steak
- Sauteed bell peppers and onions
- Provolone cheese

Directions:

1. Preheat oven to 475°F (245°C).
2. Roll out pizza dough to preferred thickness.
3. Top with sliced steak, peppers, onions, and cheese.
4. Bake for 20 minutes or until crust is golden.

Nutritional Information: 520 calories, 28g protein, 55g carbohydrates, 22g fat, 3g fiber, 70mg cholesterol, 1,200mg sodium, 360mg potassium.

Eggplant Parmesan Pizza

Yield: 4 servings | Prep Time: 25 minutes | Cook Time: 20 minutes

Ingredients:

- Pizza dough
- Tomato sauce
- Thinly sliced eggplant, roasted
- Mozzarella and Parmesan cheeses

Directions:

1. Preheat oven to 475°F (245°C).
2. Roll out pizza dough, top with sauce, eggplant, and cheeses.
3. Bake for 20 minutes or until golden and bubbly.

Nutritional Information: 430 calories, 20g protein, 52g carbohydrates, 18g fat, 4g fiber, 40mg cholesterol, 1,050mg sodium, 350mg potassium.

Fig, Prosciutto, and Blue Cheese Pizza

Yield: 4 servings | Prep Time: 20 minutes | Cook Time: 15 minutes

Ingredients:

- Pizza dough
- Fig jam
- Prosciutto
- Blue cheese

Directions:

1. Preheat oven to 475°F (245°C).
2. Roll out dough, spread fig jam, top with prosciutto and cheese.
3. Bake for 15 minutes or until crust is golden.

Nutritional Information: 410 calories, 18g protein, 48g carbohydrates, 18g fat, 2g fiber, 50mg cholesterol, 1,020mg sodium, 320mg potassium.

Sweet & Spicy Korean BBQ Pizza

Yield: 4 servings | Prep Time: 25 minutes | Cook Time: 20 minutes

Ingredients:

- Pizza dough
- Korean BBQ sauce
- Cooked chicken, shredded
- Mozzarella cheese
- Sliced green onions
- Sriracha drizzle

Directions:

1. Preheat oven to 475°F (245°C).
2. Roll out dough, spread BBQ sauce, top with chicken, cheese, and onions.
3. Bake for 20 minutes or until golden and bubbly.
4. Drizzle with sriracha before serving.

Nutritional Information: 480 calories, 22g protein, 55g carbohydrates, 20g fat, 3g fiber, 60mg cholesterol, 1,200mg sodium, 350mg potassium.

Balsamic Glazed Caprese Pizza

Yield: 4 servings | Prep Time: 20 minutes | Cook Time: 15 minutes

Ingredients:

- Pizza dough
- Fresh tomatoes, sliced
- Fresh mozzarella cheese
- Fresh basil leaves
- Balsamic glaze

Directions:

1. Preheat oven to 475°F (245°C).
2. Roll out dough, top with tomatoes and mozzarella.
3. Bake for 15 minutes or until crust is golden.
4. Top with fresh basil and balsamic glaze before serving.

Nutritional Information: 400 calories, 18g protein, 48g carbohydrates, 18g fat, 2g fiber, 40mg cholesterol, 950mg sodium, 300mg potassium.

Lobster and Sweet Corn Pizza

Yield: 4 servings | Prep Time: 30 minutes | Cook Time: 20 minutes

Ingredients:

- Pizza dough
- Lobster meat, cooked and chopped
- Fresh sweet corn kernels
- Mozzarella cheese
- Fresh dill

Directions:

1. Preheat oven to 475°F (245°C).
2. Roll out dough, top with lobster, corn, and cheese.
3. Bake for 20 minutes or until golden and bubbly.
4. Top with fresh dill before serving.

Nutritional Information: 500 calories, 25g protein, 55g carbohydrates, 20g fat, 3g fiber, 80mg cholesterol, 1,000mg sodium, 380mg potassium.

Spinach and Feta Stuffed Crust Pizza

Yield: 4 servings | Prep Time: 40 minutes | Cook Time: 25 minutes

Ingredients:

- Pizza dough
- Spinach, cooked and drained
- Feta cheese
- Tomato sauce
- Mozzarella cheese

Directions:

1. Preheat oven to 475°F (245°C).
2. Roll out dough, stuff edges with spinach and feta, fold over to seal.
3. Top with sauce and cheese.
4. Bake for 25 minutes or until crust is golden and cheese is bubbly.

Nutritional Information: 520 calories, 22g protein, 55g carbohydrates, 25g fat, 4g fiber, 60mg cholesterol, 1,150mg sodium, 360mg potassium.

Bacon and Egg Breakfast Pizza

Yield: 4 servings | Prep Time: 20 minutes | Cook Time: 15 minutes

Ingredients:

- Pizza dough
- Bacon, cooked and crumbled
- Scrambled eggs
- Cheddar cheese

Directions:

1. Preheat oven to 475°F (245°C).
2. Roll out dough, top with bacon, eggs, and cheese.
3. Bake for 15 minutes or until golden and bubbly.

Nutritional Information: 540 calories, 28g protein, 50g carbohydrates, 25g fat, 2g fiber, 200mg cholesterol, 1,200mg sodium, 350mg potassium.

Black and White Truffle Pizza

Yield: 2 servings | Prep Time: 20 minutes | Cook Time: 15 minutes

Ingredients:

- Pizza dough
- White truffle oil
- Fresh mozzarella cheese
- Black truffle shavings

Directions:

1. Preheat oven to 475°F (245°C).
2. Roll out dough, brush with truffle oil, and top with cheese.
3. Bake for 15 minutes or until crust is golden.
4. Top with truffle shavings before serving.

Nutritional Information: 420 calories, 18g protein, 48g carbohydrates, 20g fat, 2g fiber, 40mg cholesterol, 1,000mg sodium, 300mg potassium.

Taco Fiesta Pizza

Yield: 4 servings | Prep Time: 30 minutes | Cook Time: 20 minutes

Ingredients:

- Pizza dough
- Taco-seasoned ground beef, cooked and drained
- Cheddar and Monterey Jack cheeses
- Toppings: lettuce, tomatoes, olives, sour cream

Directions:

1. Preheat oven to 475°F (245°C).
2. Roll out dough, top with beef and cheeses.
3. Bake for 20 minutes or until golden and bubbly.
4. Top with lettuce, tomatoes, olives, and a drizzle of sour cream before serving.

Nutritional Information: 530 calories, 26g protein, 50g carbohydrates, 26g fat, 3g fiber, 70mg cholesterol, 1,300mg sodium, 360mg potassium.

French Ratatouille Pizza

Yield: 4 servings | Prep Time: 40 minutes | Cook Time: 20 minutes

Ingredients:

- Pizza dough
- Ratatouille (eggplant, zucchini, bell peppers, onion, and tomato)
- Mozzarella cheese
- Fresh basil leaves

Directions:

1. Preheat oven to 475°F (245°C).
2. Roll out dough, top with ratatouille and cheese.
3. Bake for 20 minutes or until golden and bubbly.
4. Top with fresh basil leaves before serving.

Nutritional Information: 520 calories, 20g protein, 80g carbohydrates, 12g fat, 10g fiber, 30mg cholesterol, 1,100mg sodium, 800mg potassium.

Sweet and Savory Apple Gorgonzola Pizza

Yield: 4 servings | Prep Time: 30 minutes | Cook Time: 15 minutes

Ingredients:

- Pizza dough
- Olive oil
- Thinly sliced apples
- Crumbled Gorgonzola cheese
- Honey

Directions:

1. Preheat oven to 475°F (245°C).
2. Roll out dough, brush with olive oil, top with apples, and Gorgonzola.
3. Bake for 15 minutes or until golden and bubbly.
4. Drizzle with honey before serving.

Nutritional Information: 540 calories, 18g protein, 78g carbohydrates, 16g fat, 4g fiber, 45mg cholesterol, 1,000mg sodium, 300mg potassium.

Rustic Butternut Squash and Sage Pizza

Yield: 4 servings | Prep Time: 40 minutes | Cook Time: 20 minutes

Ingredients:

- Pizza dough
- Roasted butternut squash, cubed
- Fresh sage leaves
- Mozzarella cheese

Directions:

1. Preheat oven to 475°F (245°C).
2. Roll out dough, top with butternut squash, sage, and cheese.
3. Bake for 20 minutes or until golden and bubbly.

Nutritional Information: 560 calories, 20g protein, 95g carbohydrates, 12g fat, 6g fiber, 30mg cholesterol, 1,100mg sodium, 700mg potassium.

Cajun Shrimp and Andouille Pizza

Yield: 4 servings | Prep Time: 30 minutes | Cook Time: 20 minutes

Ingredients:

- Pizza dough
- Olive oil
- Cajun-seasoned shrimp
- Sliced Andouille sausage
- Mozzarella cheese

Directions:

1. Preheat oven to 475°F (245°C).
2. Roll out dough, brush with olive oil, top with shrimp, Andouille, and cheese.
3. Bake for 20 minutes or until golden and bubbly.

Nutritional Information: 580 calories, 35g protein, 60g carbohydrates, 20g fat, 2g fiber, 150mg cholesterol, 1,400mg sodium, 400mg potassium.

Spicy Jerk Chicken Pizza

Yield: 4 servings | Prep Time: 30 minutes | Cook Time: 20 minutes

Ingredients:

- Pizza dough
- Jerk-seasoned chicken, cooked and cubed
- Pineapple chunks
- Mozzarella cheese

Directions:

1. Preheat oven to 475°F (245°C).
2. Roll out dough, top with chicken, pineapple, and cheese.
3. Bake for 20 minutes or until golden and bubbly.

Nutritional Information: 550 calories, 30g protein, 70g carbohydrates, 15g fat, 3g fiber, 80mg cholesterol, 1,200mg sodium, 400mg potassium.

Chocolate and Marshmallow Dessert Pizza

Yield: 6 servings | Prep Time: 25 minutes | Cook Time: 10 minutes

Ingredients:

- Pizza dough
- Chocolate hazelnut spread
- Mini marshmallows
- Crushed graham crackers

Directions:

1. Preheat oven to 475°F (245°C).
2. Roll out dough, spread a layer of chocolate hazelnut spread, sprinkle marshmallows, and crushed graham crackers.
3. Bake for 10 minutes or until marshmallows are lightly golden.

Nutritional Information: 350 calories, 5g protein, 50g carbohydrates, 15g fat, 3g fiber, 5mg cholesterol, 400mg sodium, 200mg potassium.

Middle Eastern Lamb and Feta Pizza

Yield: 4 servings | Prep Time: 45 minutes | Cook Time: 20 minutes

Ingredients:

- Pizza dough
- Ground lamb
- Tomato sauce
- Feta cheese
- Mint leaves

Directions:

1. Preheat oven to 475°F (245°C).
2. Brown ground lamb in a skillet.
3. Roll out dough, spread a layer of tomato sauce, lamb, and feta.
4. Bake for 20 minutes or until golden and bubbly.
5. Garnish with mint leaves before serving.

Nutritional Information: 540 calories, 30g protein, 58g carbohydrates, 20g fat, 3g fiber, 80mg cholesterol, 1,100mg sodium, 400mg potassium.

Smoky Pulled Pork Pizza

Yield: 4 servings | Prep Time: 30 minutes | Cook Time: 20 minutes

Ingredients:

- Pizza dough
- Pulled pork
- Barbecue sauce
- Mozzarella cheese
- Red onion

Directions:

1. Preheat oven to 475°F (245°C).
2. Roll out dough, spread a layer of barbecue sauce, pulled pork, cheese, and onion.
3. Bake for 20 minutes or until golden and bubbly.

Nutritional Information: 590 calories, 35g protein, 65g carbohydrates, 20g fat, 3g fiber, 100mg cholesterol, 1,300mg sodium, 400mg potassium.

Chicken Tikka Masala Pizza

Yield: 4 servings | Prep Time: 40 minutes | Cook Time: 20 minutes

Ingredients:

- Pizza dough
- Chicken tikka masala
- Mozzarella cheese
- Cilantro

Directions:

1. Preheat oven to 475°F (245°C).
2. Roll out dough, spread a layer of chicken tikka masala, and cheese.
3. Bake for 20 minutes or until golden and bubbly.
4. Garnish with cilantro before serving.

Nutritional Information: 540 calories, 30g protein, 58g carbohydrates, 20g fat, 3g fiber, 80mg cholesterol, 1,200mg sodium, 400mg potassium.

Quattro Formaggi (Four Cheese) Pizza

Yield: 4 servings | Prep Time: 30 minutes | Cook Time: 20 minutes

Ingredients:

- Pizza dough
- Mozzarella cheese
- Parmesan cheese
- Gorgonzola cheese
- Fontina cheese

Directions:

1. Preheat oven to 475°F (245°C).
2. Roll out dough, spread the four types of cheese evenly over the dough.
3. Bake for 20 minutes or until golden and bubbly.

Nutritional Information: 530 calories, 30g protein, 58g carbohydrates, 20g fat, 3g fiber, 80mg cholesterol, 1,200mg sodium, 200mg potassium.

Spicy Italian Sausage Pizza

Yield: 4 servings | Prep Time: 30 minutes | Cook Time: 20 minutes

Ingredients:

- Pizza dough
- Spicy Italian sausage
- Tomato sauce
- Mozzarella cheese
- Red pepper flakes

Directions:

1. Preheat oven to 475°F (245°C).
2. Brown sausage in a skillet.
3. Roll out dough, spread a layer of tomato sauce, sausage, cheese, and a sprinkle of red pepper flakes.
4. Bake for 20 minutes or until golden and bubbly.

Nutritional Information: 600 calories, 30g protein, 55g carbohydrates, 25g fat, 2g fiber, 80mg cholesterol, 1,300mg sodium, 350mg potassium.

Caramelized Onion and Goat Cheese Pizza

Yield: 4 servings | Prep Time: 40 minutes | Cook Time: 20 minutes

Ingredients:

- Pizza dough
- Caramelized onions
- Goat cheese
- Fresh thyme

Directions:

1. Preheat oven to 475°F (245°C).
2. Roll out dough, spread a layer of caramelized onions, and goat cheese.
3. Bake for 20 minutes or until golden and bubbly.
4. Garnish with fresh thyme before serving.

Nutritional Information: 520 calories, 22g protein, 58g carbohydrates, 22g fat, 4g fiber, 60mg cholesterol, 1,000mg sodium, 300mg potassium.

Wild Mushroom and Thyme Pizza

Yield: 4 servings | Prep Time: 40 minutes | Cook Time: 20 minutes

Ingredients:

- Pizza dough
- Mixed wild mushrooms
- Olive oil
- Fresh thyme
- Mozzarella cheese

Directions:

1. Preheat oven to 475°F (245°C).
2. Sauté mushrooms in olive oil until golden.
3. Roll out dough, spread a layer of mushrooms, and mozzarella cheese.
4. Bake for 20 minutes or until golden and bubbly.
5. Garnish with fresh thyme before serving.

Nutritional Information: 560 calories, 25g protein, 60g carbohydrates, 24g fat, 4g fiber, 60mg cholesterol, 1,000mg sodium, 400mg potassium.

Pear and Gorgonzola Pizza

Yield: 4 servings | Prep Time: 30 minutes | Cook Time: 20 minutes

Ingredients:

- Pizza dough
- Sliced pears
- Gorgonzola cheese
- Fresh arugula

Directions:

1. Preheat oven to 475°F (245°C).
2. Roll out dough, spread a layer of pears, and gorgonzola cheese.
3. Bake for 20 minutes or until golden and bubbly.
4. Garnish with fresh arugula before serving.

Nutritional Information: 490 calories, 22g protein, 55g carbohydrates, 20g fat, 4g fiber, 40mg cholesterol, 1,100mg sodium, 350mg potassium.

Clam and Garlic Pizza

Yield: 4 servings | Prep Time: 30 minutes | Cook Time: 20 minutes

Ingredients:

- Pizza dough
- Clams in shell
- Garlic
- Olive oil
- Mozzarella cheese
- Fresh parsley

Directions:

1. Preheat oven to 475°F (245°C).
2. Sauté clams and garlic in olive oil until clams open.
3. Roll out dough, spread a layer of the clam and garlic mixture, and mozzarella cheese.
4. Bake for 20 minutes or until golden and bubbly.
5. Garnish with fresh parsley before serving.

Nutritional Information: 540 calories, 28g protein, 55g carbohydrates, 22g fat, 2g fiber, 80mg cholesterol, 1,200mg sodium, 400mg potassium.

Chili Cheese Dog Pizza

Yield: 4 servings | Prep Time: 30 minutes | Cook Time: 20 minutes

Ingredients:

- Pizza dough
- Chili (no beans)
- Hot dogs
- Cheddar cheese
- Onions

Directions:

1. Preheat oven to 475°F (245°C).
2. Roll out dough, spread a layer of chili, sliced hot dogs, cheese, and onions.
3. Bake for 20 minutes or until golden and bubbly.

Nutritional Information: 680 calories, 32g protein, 60g carbohydrates, 36g fat, 4g fiber, 85mg cholesterol, 1,500mg sodium, 400mg potassium.

Provolone and Roasted Pepper Pizza

Yield: 4 servings | Prep Time: 30 minutes | Cook Time: 20 minutes

Ingredients:

- Pizza dough
- Provolone cheese
- Roasted red peppers
- Olive oil
- Fresh basil

Directions:

1. Preheat oven to 475°F (245°C).
2. Roll out dough, spread a layer of provolone cheese, and roasted peppers.
3. Bake for 20 minutes or until golden and bubbly.
4. Garnish with fresh basil before serving.

Nutritional Information: 570 calories, 28g protein, 58g carbohydrates, 26g fat, 3g fiber, 70mg cholesterol, 1,100mg sodium, 350mg potassium.

Buffalo Mozzarella and Basil Pizza

Yield: 4 servings | Prep Time: 30 minutes | Cook Time: 20 minutes

Ingredients:

- Pizza dough
- Buffalo mozzarella
- Tomato sauce
- Fresh basil

Directions:

1. Preheat oven to 475°F (245°C).
2. Roll out dough, spread a layer of tomato sauce, and buffalo mozzarella.
3. Bake for 20 minutes or until golden and bubbly.
4. Garnish with fresh basil before serving.

Nutritional Information: 520 calories, 25g protein, 55g carbohydrates, 22g fat, 3g fiber, 60mg cholesterol, 1,000mg sodium, 300mg potassium.

Sweet Potato and Kale Pizza

Yield: 4 servings | Prep Time: 40 minutes | Cook Time: 20 minutes

Ingredients:

- Pizza dough
- Sweet potatoes
- Kale
- Olive oil
- Mozzarella cheese

Directions:

1. Preheat oven to 475°F (245°C).
2. Sauté sweet potatoes and kale in olive oil until tender.
3. Roll out dough, spread a layer of the sweet potato and kale mixture, and mozzarella cheese.
4. Bake for 20 minutes or until golden and bubbly.

Nutritional Information: 540 calories, 23g protein, 65g carbohydrates, 20g fat, 6g fiber, 50mg cholesterol, 1,000mg sodium, 500mg potassium.

Roasted Garlic and White Sauce Pizza

Yield: 4 servings | Prep Time: 40 minutes | Cook Time: 20 minutes

Ingredients:

- Pizza dough
- Roasted garlic
- White sauce (alfredo or béchamel)
- Mozzarella cheese
- Fresh parsley

Directions:

1. Preheat oven to 475°F (245°C).
2. Roll out dough, spread a layer of white sauce, roasted garlic, and mozzarella cheese.
3. Bake for 20 minutes or until golden and bubbly.
4. Garnish with fresh parsley before serving.

Nutritional Information: 600 calories, 22g protein, 60g carbohydrates, 26g fat, 3g fiber, 60mg cholesterol, 1,100mg sodium, 350mg potassium.

Black Olive and Feta Cheese Pizza

Yield: 4 servings | Prep Time: 30 minutes | Cook Time: 20 minutes

Ingredients:

- Pizza dough
- Black olives
- Feta cheese
- Tomato sauce
- Fresh parsley

Directions:

1. Preheat oven to 475°F (245°C).
2. Roll out dough, spread a layer of tomato sauce, black olives, and feta cheese.
3. Bake for 20 minutes or until golden and bubbly.
4. Garnish with fresh parsley before serving.

Nutritional Information: 540 calories, 20g protein, 60g carbohydrates, 24g fat, 4g fiber, 45mg cholesterol, 1,300mg sodium, 350mg potassium.

BBQ Pulled Pork Pizza

Yield: 4 servings | Prep Time: 30 minutes | Cook Time: 20 minutes

Ingredients:

- Pizza dough
- BBQ pulled pork
- BBQ sauce
- Mozzarella cheese
- Red onion

Directions:

1. Preheat oven to 475°F (245°C).
2. Roll out dough, spread a layer of BBQ sauce, BBQ pulled pork, mozzarella cheese, and thinly sliced red onion.
3. Bake for 20 minutes or until golden and bubbly.

Nutritional Information: 720 calories, 34g protein, 65g carbohydrates, 34g fat, 3g fiber, 85mg cholesterol, 1,500mg sodium, 400mg potassium.

Fresh Tomato and Basil Pizza

Yield: 4 servings | Prep Time: 30 minutes | Cook Time: 20 minutes

Ingredients:

- Pizza dough
- Fresh tomatoes
- Fresh basil
- Mozzarella cheese
- Olive oil

Directions:

1. Preheat oven to 475°F (245°C).
2. Roll out dough, arrange a layer of sliced fresh tomatoes, and sprinkle with mozzarella cheese.
3. Bake for 20 minutes or until golden and bubbly.
4. Garnish with fresh basil before serving.

Nutritional Information: 510 calories, 24g protein, 55g carbohydrates, 22g fat, 3g fiber, 60mg cholesterol, 1,000mg sodium, 300mg potassium.

Roasted Brussels Sprouts and Bacon Pizza

Yield: 4 servings | Prep Time: 40 minutes | Cook Time: 20 minutes

Ingredients:

- Pizza dough
- Brussels sprouts
- Bacon
- Mozzarella cheese
- Olive oil

Directions:

1. Preheat oven to 475°F (245°C).
2. Roast Brussels sprouts in the oven with a bit of olive oil until tender.
3. Roll out dough, spread a layer of the roasted Brussels sprouts, cooked and crumbled bacon, and mozzarella cheese.
4. Bake for 20 minutes or until golden and bubbly.

Nutritional Information: 630 calories, 30g protein, 58g carbohydrates, 30g fat, 5g fiber, 80mg cholesterol, 1,200mg sodium, 450mg potassium.

Spicy Tandoori Chicken Pizza

Yield: 4 servings | Prep Time: 40 minutes | Cook Time: 20 minutes

Ingredients:

- Pizza dough
- Tandoori chicken
- Mozzarella cheese
- Cilantro
- Red onion

Directions:

1. Preheat oven to 475°F (245°C).
2. Roll out dough, spread a layer of the tandoori chicken, mozzarella cheese, and thinly sliced red onion.
3. Bake for 20 minutes or until golden and bubbly.
4. Garnish with fresh cilantro before serving.

Nutritional Information: 680 calories, 35g protein, 60g carbohydrates, 30g fat, 3g fiber, 85mg cholesterol, 1,300mg sodium, 400mg potassium.

Bacon Cheeseburger Pizza

Yield: 4 servings | Prep Time: 30 minutes | Cook Time: 20 minutes

Ingredients:

- Pizza dough
- Ground beef
- Bacon
- Cheddar cheese
- Tomato sauce
- Pickles
- Mustard

Directions:

1. Preheat oven to 475°F (245°C).
2. Cook ground beef and bacon, set aside.
3. Roll out dough, spread a layer of tomato sauce, ground beef, bacon, and cheddar cheese.
4. Bake for 20 minutes or until golden and bubbly.
5. Top with pickles and a drizzle of mustard before serving.

Nutritional Information: 710 calories, 35g protein, 55g carbohydrates, 40g fat, 3g fiber, 105mg cholesterol, 1,500mg sodium, 500mg potassium.

French Fry and Gravy Pizza

Yield: 4 servings | Prep Time: 30 minutes | Cook Time: 25 minutes

Ingredients:

- Pizza dough
- French fries
- Cheese curds
- Gravy

Directions:

1. Preheat oven to 475°F (245°C).
2. Roll out dough and bake for 5 minutes.
3. Top baked dough with cooked French fries and cheese curds, then drizzle with gravy.
4. Bake for another 20 minutes or until golden and bubbly.

Nutritional Information: 690 calories, 20g protein, 85g carbohydrates, 30g fat, 6g fiber, 60mg cholesterol, 1,700mg sodium, 500mg potassium.

Chipotle Chicken Pizza

Yield: 4 servings | Prep Time: 30 minutes | Cook Time: 20 minutes

Ingredients:

- Pizza dough
- Chicken breast
- Chipotle sauce
- Red onion
- Mozzarella cheese

Directions:

1. Preheat oven to 475°F (245°C).
2. Cook chicken breast and slice thinly, set aside.
3. Roll out dough, spread a layer of chipotle sauce, chicken slices, red onion, and mozzarella cheese.
4. Bake for 20 minutes or until golden and bubbly.

Nutritional Information: 630 calories, 33g protein, 60g carbohydrates, 28g fat, 3g fiber, 85mg cholesterol, 1,200mg sodium, 400mg potassium.

Prosciutto and Fig Pizza

Yield: 4 servings | Prep Time: 30 minutes | Cook Time: 20 minutes

Ingredients:

- Pizza dough
- Prosciutto
- Fresh figs
- Goat cheese
- Arugula

Directions:

1. Preheat oven to 475°F (245°C).
2. Roll out dough, spread a layer of prosciutto, sliced figs, and goat cheese.
3. Bake for 20 minutes or until golden and bubbly.
4. Top with fresh arugula before serving.

Nutritional Information: 590 calories, 28g protein, 60g carbohydrates, 27g fat, 4g fiber, 75mg cholesterol, 1,200mg sodium, 350mg potassium.

Sausage and Rapini Pizza

Yield: 4 servings | Prep Time: 30 minutes | Cook Time: 20 minutes

Ingredients:

- Pizza dough
- Italian sausage
- Rapini
- Mozzarella cheese
- Red chili flakes

Directions:

1. Preheat oven to 475°F (245°C).
2. Cook Italian sausage, set aside.
3. Blanch rapini in boiling water for 2 minutes, then drain.
4. Roll out dough, spread a layer of sausage, blanched rapini, and mozzarella cheese.
5. Sprinkle with red chili flakes and bake for 20 minutes or until golden and bubbly.

Nutritional Information: 630 calories, 32g protein, 60g carbohydrates, 29g fat, 5g fiber, 85mg cholesterol, 1,300mg sodium, 450mg potassium.

Caramelized Pear and Blue Cheese Pizza

Yield: 4 servings | Prep Time: 40 minutes | Cook Time: 20 minutes

Ingredients:

- Pizza dough
- Pears
- Blue cheese
- Butter
- Brown sugar

Directions:

1. Preheat oven to 475°F (245°C).
2. In a pan, melt butter and add brown sugar. Once melted, add sliced pears and cook until caramelized.
3. Roll out dough, spread a layer of caramelized pears, and top with crumbled blue cheese.
4. Bake for 20 minutes or until golden and bubbly.

Nutritional Information: 500 calories, 12g protein, 60g carbohydrates, 25g fat, 4g fiber, 30mg cholesterol, 800mg sodium, 200mg potassium.

Zucchini and Herbed Ricotta Pizza

Yield: 4 servings | Prep Time: 30 minutes | Cook Time: 20 minutes

Ingredients:

- Pizza dough
- Zucchini
- Ricotta cheese
- Fresh herbs (basil, oregano, thyme)

Directions:

1. Preheat oven to 475°F (245°C).
2. Slice zucchini thinly and mix ricotta cheese with chopped fresh herbs.
3. Roll out dough, spread a layer of herbed ricotta, and top with zucchini slices.
4. Bake for 20 minutes or until golden and bubbly.

Nutritional Information: 450 calories, 15g protein, 65g carbohydrates, 15g fat, 5g fiber, 30mg cholesterol, 800mg sodium, 300mg potassium.

Pumpkin and Sage Pizza

Yield: 4 servings | Prep Time: 40 minutes | Cook Time: 20 minutes

Ingredients:

- Pizza dough
- Pumpkin puree
- Fresh sage
- Mozzarella cheese
- Nutmeg

Directions:

1. Preheat oven to 475°F (245°C).
2. Roll out dough, spread a layer of pumpkin puree, sprinkle fresh sage, and top with mozzarella cheese.
3. Sprinkle with nutmeg and bake for 20 minutes or until golden and bubbly.

Nutritional Information: 400 calories, 15g protein, 65g carbohydrates, 10g fat, 6g fiber, 25mg cholesterol, 800mg sodium, 400mg potassium.

Italian Salami and Red Onion Pizza

Yield: 4 servings | Prep Time: 30 minutes | Cook Time: 20 minutes

Ingredients:

- Pizza dough
- Italian salami
- Red onion
- Mozzarella cheese
- Tomato sauce

Directions:

1. Preheat oven to 475°F (245°C).
2. Roll out dough, spread a layer of tomato sauce, add Italian salami slices and thin red onion slices.
3. Top with mozzarella cheese and bake for 20 minutes or until golden and bubbly.

Nutritional Information: 600 calories, 25g protein, 60g carbohydrates, 30g fat, 4g fiber, 60mg cholesterol, 1,500mg sodium, 300mg potassium.

Chicken Alfredo Pizza

Yield: 4 servings | Prep Time: 40 minutes | Cook Time: 20 minutes

Ingredients:

- Pizza dough
- Chicken breast
- Alfredo sauce
- Mozzarella cheese
- Parmesan cheese

Directions:

1. Preheat oven to 475°F (245°C).
2. Cook chicken breast and slice thinly, set aside.
3. Roll out dough, spread a layer of Alfredo sauce, add chicken slices, and top with mozzarella and Parmesan cheese.
4. Bake for 20 minutes or until golden and bubbly.

Nutritional Information: 680 calories, 30g protein, 60g carbohydrates, 35g fat, 3g fiber, 85mg cholesterol, 1,300mg sodium, 350mg potassium.

Recipe's Name: Anchovy and Capers Pizza

Yield: 4 servings | Prep Time: 15 minutes | Cook Time: 15 minutes

Ingredients:

- Pizza dough
- Anchovy fillets
- Capers
- Mozzarella cheese
- Tomato sauce

Directions:

1. Preheat oven to 475°F (245°C).
2. Roll out dough, spread a layer of tomato sauce, add anchovy fillets and capers.
3. Top with mozzarella cheese and bake for 15 minutes or until golden and bubbly.

Nutritional Information: 560 calories, 25g protein, 60g carbohydrates, 25g fat, 5g fiber, 45mg cholesterol, 1,700mg sodium, 500mg potassium.

Asparagus and Hollandaise Pizza

Yield: 4 servings | Prep Time: 30 minutes | Cook Time: 20 minutes

Ingredients:

- Pizza dough
- Asparagus spears
- Hollandaise sauce
- Mozzarella cheese

Directions:

1. Preheat oven to 475°F (245°C).
2. Roll out dough, spread a layer of Hollandaise sauce, add asparagus spears.
3. Top with mozzarella cheese and bake for 20 minutes or until golden and bubbly.

Nutritional Information: 600 calories, 20g protein, 65g carbohydrates, 30g fat, 5g fiber, 90mg cholesterol, 1,000mg sodium, 400mg potassium.

Buffalo Cauliflower Pizza

Yield: 4 servings | Prep Time: 40 minutes | Cook Time: 20 minutes

Ingredients:

- Pizza dough
- Cauliflower florets
- Buffalo sauce
- Blue cheese
- Mozzarella cheese

Directions:

1. Preheat oven to 475°F (245°C).
2. Toss cauliflower florets in buffalo sauce and roast separately for 15 minutes.
3. Roll out dough, spread a layer of buffalo sauce, add roasted cauliflower.
4. Top with mozzarella and blue cheese and bake for 20 minutes or until golden and bubbly.

Nutritional Information: 500 calories, 20g protein, 65g carbohydrates, 20g fat, 6g fiber, 40mg cholesterol, 1,500mg sodium, 600mg potassium.

Bacon Jalapeno Popper Pizza

Yield: 4 servings | Prep Time: 20 minutes | Cook Time: 20 minutes

Ingredients:

- Pizza dough
- Bacon
- Jalapenos
- Cream cheese
- Mozzarella cheese

Directions:

1. Preheat oven to 475°F (245°C).
2. Cook bacon until crispy, roll out dough, spread a layer of cream cheese, add bacon and sliced jalapenos.
3. Top with mozzarella cheese and bake for 20 minutes or until golden and bubbly.

Nutritional Information: 650 calories, 25g protein, 60g carbohydrates, 35g fat, 3g fiber, 80mg cholesterol, 1,400mg sodium, 300mg potassium.

Crab Rangoon Pizza

Yield: 4 servings | Prep Time: 30 minutes | Cook Time: 20 minutes

Ingredients:

- Pizza dough
- Crab meat
- Cream cheese
- Scallions
- Mozzarella cheese
- Sweet and sour sauce

Directions:

1. Preheat oven to 475°F (245°C).
2. Mix crab meat with cream cheese and chopped scallions, roll out dough, spread a layer of the crab mixture.
3. Top with mozzarella cheese and bake for 20 minutes or until golden and bubbly.
4. Drizzle with sweet and sour sauce before serving.

Nutritional Information: 600 calories, 30g protein, 65g carbohydrates, 25g fat, 3g fiber, 85mg cholesterol, 1,000mg sodium, 400mg potassium.

Grilled Chicken and Pesto Pizza

Yield: 4 servings | Prep Time: 20 minutes | Cook Time: 15 minutes

Ingredients:

- Pizza dough
- Grilled chicken breast
- Pesto sauce
- Mozzarella cheese

Directions:

1. Preheat oven to 475°F (245°C).
2. Roll out dough, spread a layer of pesto sauce, add sliced grilled chicken.
3. Top with mozzarella cheese and bake for 15 minutes or until golden and bubbly.

Nutritional Information: 550 calories, 30g protein, 55g carbohydrates, 25g fat, 4g fiber, 70mg cholesterol, 950mg sodium, 600mg potassium.

Shaved Asparagus and Parmesan Pizza

Yield: 4 servings | Prep Time: 20 minutes | Cook Time: 20 minutes

Ingredients:

- Pizza dough
- Asparagus spears
- Parmesan cheese
- Olive oil

Directions:

1. Preheat oven to 475°F (245°C).
2. Roll out dough, drizzle with olive oil, add shaved asparagus.
3. Top with shaved parmesan cheese and bake for 20 minutes or until golden and bubbly.

Nutritional Information: 450 calories, 20g protein, 60g carbohydrates, 15g fat, 6g fiber, 25mg cholesterol, 800mg sodium, 500mg potassium.

Cherry Tomato and Mozzarella Pizza

Yield: 4 servings | Prep Time: 10 minutes | Cook Time: 15 minutes

Ingredients:

- Pizza dough
- Cherry tomatoes
- Mozzarella cheese
- Basil leaves
- Olive oil

Directions:

1. Preheat oven to 475°F (245°C).
2. Roll out dough, drizzle with olive oil, add halved cherry tomatoes.
3. Top with mozzarella cheese and bake for 15 minutes or until golden and bubbly.
4. Garnish with fresh basil leaves before serving.

Nutritional Information: 500 calories, 25g protein, 60g carbohydrates, 20g fat, 4g fiber, 45mg cholesterol, 800mg sodium, 400mg potassium.

Brie and Cranberry Pizza

Yield: 4 servings | Prep Time: 10 minutes | Cook Time: 15 minutes

Ingredients:

- Pizza dough
- Brie cheese
- Cranberry sauce
- Arugula leaves

Directions:

1. Preheat oven to 475°F (245°C).
2. Roll out dough, spread a layer of cranberry sauce, add sliced brie.
3. Bake for 15 minutes or until golden and bubbly.
4. Garnish with fresh arugula leaves before serving.

Nutritional Information: 600 calories, 25g protein, 65g carbohydrates, 30g fat, 5g fiber, 90mg cholesterol, 1,000mg sodium, 400mg potassium.

Beer Cheese and Bratwurst Pizza

Yield: 4 servings | Prep Time: 25 minutes | Cook Time: 20 minutes

Ingredients:

- Pizza dough
- Bratwurst
- Beer cheese
- Red onion
- Mozzarella cheese

Directions:

1. Preheat oven to 475°F (245°C).
2. Cook bratwurst until browned, slice, roll out dough, spread a layer of beer cheese, add bratwurst and thinly sliced red onion.
3. Top with mozzarella cheese and bake for 20 minutes or until golden and bubbly.

Nutritional Information: 700 calories, 30g protein, 60g carbohydrates, 35g fat, 4g fiber, 90mg cholesterol, 1,500mg sodium, 500mg potassium.

Sesame Chicken Pizza

Yield: 4 servings | Prep Time: 20 minutes | Cook Time: 20 minutes

Ingredients:

- Pizza dough
- Sesame chicken
- Mozzarella cheese
- Sesame seeds
- Spring onions

Directions:

1. Preheat oven to 475°F (245°C).
2. Roll out dough, spread a layer of sesame chicken, and top with mozzarella cheese.
3. Bake for 20 minutes or until golden and bubbly.
4. Sprinkle with sesame seeds and freshly chopped spring onions before serving.

Nutritional Information: 600 calories, 30g protein, 65g carbohydrates, 25g fat, 5g fiber, 75mg cholesterol, 1,000mg sodium, 500mg potassium.

Creamy Leek and Pancetta Pizza

Yield: 4 servings | Prep Time: 20 minutes | Cook Time: 20 minutes

Ingredients:

- Pizza dough
- Leeks
- Pancetta
- Cream cheese
- Mozzarella cheese

Directions:

1. Preheat oven to 475°F (245°C).
2. Roll out dough, spread a layer of cream cheese, add sautéed leeks and crispy pancetta.
3. Top with mozzarella cheese and bake for 20 minutes or until golden and bubbly.

Nutritional Information: 650 calories, 30g protein, 60g carbohydrates, 35g fat, 4g fiber, 85mg cholesterol, 1,100mg sodium, 500mg potassium.

Kalamata Olive and Greek Feta Pizza

Yield: 4 servings | Prep Time: 15 minutes | Cook Time: 20 minutes

Ingredients:

- Pizza dough
- Kalamata olives
- Greek feta
- Tomato sauce
- Oregano

Directions:

1. Preheat oven to 475°F (245°C).
2. Roll out dough, spread a layer of tomato sauce, add chopped Kalamata olives, and crumbled Greek feta.
3. Sprinkle with oregano and bake for 20 minutes or until golden and bubbly.

Nutritional Information: 550 calories, 25g protein, 60g carbohydrates, 25g fat, 5g fiber, 60mg cholesterol, 1,500mg sodium, 400mg potassium.

Italian Meatball and Ricotta Pizza

Yield: 4 servings | Prep Time: 25 minutes | Cook Time: 20 minutes

Ingredients:

- Pizza dough
- Italian meatballs
- Ricotta cheese
- Tomato sauce
- Mozzarella cheese

Directions:

1. Preheat oven to 475°F (245°C).
2. Roll out dough, spread a layer of tomato sauce, add sliced Italian meatballs, and dollops of ricotta cheese.
3. Top with mozzarella cheese and bake for 20 minutes or until golden and bubbly.

Nutritional Information: 700 calories, 35g protein, 65g carbohydrates, 35g fat, 5g fiber, 90mg cholesterol, 1,500mg sodium, 500mg potassium.

Pecan, Pear, and Gorgonzola Pizza

Yield: 4 servings | Prep Time: 15 minutes | Cook Time: 20 minutes

Ingredients:

- Pizza dough
- Pecans
- Pear
- Gorgonzola cheese
- Honey

Directions:

1. Preheat oven to 475°F (245°C).
2. Roll out dough, add sliced pears, chopped pecans, and crumbled Gorgonzola cheese.
3. Bake for 20 minutes or until golden and bubbly.
4. Drizzle with honey before serving.

Nutritional Information: 650 calories, 20g protein, 70g carbohydrates, 35g fat, 6g fiber, 60mg cholesterol, 800mg sodium, 500mg potassium.

Spaghetti and Meatball Pizza

Yield: 4 servings | Prep Time: 30 minutes | Cook Time: 20 minutes

Ingredients:

- Pizza dough
- Spaghetti
- Meatballs
- Tomato sauce
- Mozzarella cheese
- Grated Parmesan cheese

Directions:

1. Preheat oven to 475°F (245°C).
2. Roll out dough, spread a layer of tomato sauce, add cooked spaghetti, and meatballs.
3. Top with mozzarella cheese and bake for 20 minutes or until golden and bubbly.
4. Sprinkle with grated Parmesan cheese before serving.

Nutritional Information: 720 calories, 35g protein, 80g carbohydrates, 30g fat, 6g fiber, 90mg cholesterol, 1,200mg sodium, 500mg potassium.

Chicken, Spinach, and Artichoke Pizza

Yield: 4 servings | Prep Time: 20 minutes | Cook Time: 20 minutes

Ingredients:

- Pizza dough
- Chicken
- Spinach
- Artichoke hearts
- Alfredo sauce
- Mozzarella cheese

Directions:

1. Preheat oven to 475°F (245°C).
2. Roll out dough, spread a layer of Alfredo sauce, add cooked chicken, spinach, and artichoke hearts.
3. Top with mozzarella cheese and bake for 20 minutes or until golden and bubbly.

Nutritional Information: 650 calories, 35g protein, 60g carbohydrates, 30g fat, 5g fiber, 85mg cholesterol, 1,100mg sodium, 500mg potassium.

Italian Sausage and Roasted Red Pepper Pizza

Yield: 4 servings | Prep Time: 20 minutes | Cook Time: 20 minutes

Ingredients:

- Pizza dough
- Italian sausage
- Roasted red peppers
- Tomato sauce
- Mozzarella cheese

Directions:

1. Preheat oven to 475°F (245°C).
2. Roll out dough, spread a layer of tomato sauce, add cooked Italian sausage, and roasted red peppers.
3. Top with mozzarella cheese and bake for 20 minutes or until golden and bubbly.

Nutritional Information: 700 calories, 35g protein, 65g carbohydrates, 35g fat, 4g fiber, 90mg cholesterol, 1,500mg sodium, 600mg potassium.

Broccoli and Cheddar Pizza

Yield: 4 servings | Prep Time: 15 minutes | Cook Time: 20 minutes

Ingredients:

- Pizza dough
- Broccoli
- Cheddar cheese
- Alfredo sauce

Directions:

1. Preheat oven to 475°F (245°C).
2. Roll out dough, spread a layer of Alfredo sauce, add chopped broccoli.
3. Top with cheddar cheese and bake for 20 minutes or until golden and bubbly.

Nutritional Information: 600 calories, 25g protein, 60g carbohydrates, 30g fat, 6g fiber, 75mg cholesterol, 1,100mg sodium, 400mg potassium.

Garlic Prawn and Fresh Chili Pizza

Yield: 4 servings | Prep Time: 20 minutes | Cook Time: 20 minutes

Ingredients:

- Pizza dough
- Prawns
- Fresh chili
- Garlic
- Tomato sauce
- Mozzarella cheese

Directions:

1. Preheat oven to 475°F (245°C).
2. Roll out dough, spread a layer of tomato sauce, add garlic prawns, and fresh chopped chili.
3. Top with mozzarella cheese and bake for 20 minutes or until golden and bubbly.

Nutritional Information: 650 calories, 35g protein, 60g carbohydrates, 30g fat, 4g fiber, 200mg cholesterol, 1,200mg sodium, 500mg potassium.

Squid Ink and Seafood Pizza

Yield: 4 servings | Prep Time: 40 minutes | Cook Time: 20 minutes

Ingredients:

- Pizza dough
- Squid ink
- Assorted seafood (shrimp, squid, clams)
- Tomato sauce
- Mozzarella cheese
- Fresh parsley

Directions:

1. Preheat oven to 475°F (245°C).
2. Mix squid ink with the pizza dough, roll it out, then spread a layer of tomato sauce.
3. Add assorted seafood and top with mozzarella cheese.
4. Bake for 20 minutes or until golden and bubbly.
5. Garnish with fresh parsley before serving.

Nutritional Information: 680 calories, 35g protein, 60g carbohydrates, 30g fat, 5g fiber, 160mg cholesterol, 1,300mg sodium, 450mg potassium.

Turkey and Cranberry Thanksgiving Pizza

Yield: 4 servings | Prep Time: 20 minutes | Cook Time: 20 minutes

Ingredients:

- Pizza dough
- Turkey breast
- Cranberry sauce
- Mozzarella cheese
- Fresh rosemary

Directions:

1. Preheat oven to 475°F (245°C).
2. Roll out dough, spread a layer of cranberry sauce, add cooked turkey breast.
3. Top with mozzarella cheese and bake for 20 minutes or until golden and bubbly.
4. Garnish with fresh rosemary before serving.

Nutritional Information: 690 calories, 45g protein, 70g carbohydrates, 25g fat, 4g fiber, 90mg cholesterol, 1,200mg sodium, 550mg potassium.

Roasted Potato and Rosemary Pizza

Yield: 4 servings | Prep Time: 30 minutes | Cook Time: 20 minutes

Ingredients:

- Pizza dough
- Roasted potatoes
- Fresh rosemary
- Garlic olive oil
- Mozzarella cheese

Directions:

1. Preheat oven to 475°F (245°C).
2. Roll out dough, spread a thin layer of garlic olive oil, add roasted potatoes.
3. Sprinkle fresh rosemary and top with mozzarella cheese.
4. Bake for 20 minutes or until golden and bubbly.

Nutritional Information: 600 calories, 20g protein, 85g carbohydrates, 25g fat, 6g fiber, 45mg cholesterol, 1,000mg sodium, 700mg potassium.

Chorizo and Manchego Pizza

Yield: 4 servings | Prep Time: 15 minutes | Cook Time: 20 minutes

Ingredients:

- Pizza dough
- Chorizo sausage
- Manchego cheese
- Tomato sauce
- Fresh oregano

Directions:

1. Preheat oven to 475°F (245°C).
2. Roll out dough, spread a layer of tomato sauce, add sliced chorizo sausage.
3. Top with Manchego cheese and bake for 20 minutes or until golden and bubbly.
4. Sprinkle with fresh oregano before serving.

Nutritional Information: 750 calories, 35g protein, 65g carbohydrates, 40g fat, 4g fiber, 90mg cholesterol, 1,600mg sodium, 500mg potassium.

Brisket and Pickles Pizza

Yield: 4 servings | Prep Time: 20 minutes | Cook Time: 20 minutes

Ingredients:

- Pizza dough
- Brisket
- Pickles
- Barbecue sauce
- Mozzarella cheese

Directions:

1. Preheat oven to 475°F (245°C).
2. Roll out dough, spread a layer of barbecue sauce, add cooked brisket.
3. Top with mozzarella cheese and bake for 20 minutes or until golden and bubbly.
4. Add sliced pickles before serving.

Nutritional Information: 700 calories, 35g protein, 60g carbohydrates, 35g fat, 5g fiber, 90mg cholesterol, 1,500mg sodium, 400mg potassium.

Mexican Street Corn Pizza

Yield: 4 servings | Prep Time: 30 minutes | Cook Time: 20 minutes

Ingredients:

- Pizza dough
- Corn kernels
- Cotija cheese
- Cilantro
- Chili powder
- Lime
- Mozzarella cheese
- Sour cream

Directions:

1. Preheat oven to 475°F (245°C).
2. Roll out the dough, add the corn and mozzarella cheese.
3. Sprinkle with chili powder and crumbled cotija cheese.
4. Bake for 20 minutes or until golden and bubbly.
5. Top with fresh cilantro, a squeeze of lime, and a drizzle of sour cream before serving.

Nutritional Information: 640 calories, 25g protein, 85g carbohydrates, 25g fat, 6g fiber, 45mg cholesterol, 1,000mg sodium, 400mg potassium.

Lebanese Lamb and Pomegranate Pizza

Yield: 4 servings | Prep Time: 30 minutes | Cook Time: 20 minutes

Ingredients:

- Pizza dough
- Ground lamb
- Pomegranate seeds
- Feta cheese
- Fresh mint
- Lemon zest

Directions:

1. Preheat oven to 475°F (245°C).
2. Roll out the dough, add cooked ground lamb and feta cheese.
3. Bake for 20 minutes or until golden and bubbly.
4. Top with pomegranate seeds, fresh mint, and lemon zest before serving.

Nutritional Information: 720 calories, 30g protein, 70g carbohydrates, 35g fat, 4g fiber, 90mg cholesterol, 1,200mg sodium, 500mg potassium.

Provolone, Mushroom, and Truffle Oil Pizza

Yield: 4 servings | Prep Time: 15 minutes | Cook Time: 20 minutes

Ingredients:

- Pizza dough
- Provolone cheese
- Mushrooms
- Truffle oil
- Parsley

Directions:

1. Preheat oven to 475°F (245°C).
2. Roll out the dough, add sliced mushrooms and provolone cheese.
3. Bake for 20 minutes or until golden and bubbly.
4. Drizzle with truffle oil and sprinkle with fresh parsley before serving.

Nutritional Information: 670 calories, 30g protein, 70g carbohydrates, 30g fat, 5g fiber, 60mg cholesterol, 1,100mg sodium, 450mg potassium.

Chicken, Brie, and Apple Pizza

Yield: 4 servings | Prep Time: 20 minutes | Cook Time: 20 minutes

Ingredients:

- Pizza dough
- Chicken breast
- Brie cheese
- Apple slices
- Arugula

Directions:

1. Preheat oven to 475°F (245°C).
2. Roll out the dough, add cooked chicken breast, brie cheese, and apple slices.
3. Bake for 20 minutes or until golden and bubbly.
4. Top with fresh arugula before serving.

Nutritional Information: 690 calories, 35g protein, 70g carbohydrates, 30g fat, 5g fiber, 75mg cholesterol, 1,100mg sodium, 450mg potassium.

Bacon, Lettuce, and Tomato Pizza

Yield: 4 servings | Prep Time: 15 minutes | Cook Time: 20 minutes

Ingredients:

- Pizza dough
- Bacon
- Lettuce
- Tomato
- Mayo

Directions:

1. Preheat oven to 475°F (245°C).
2. Roll out the dough, add cooked bacon and bake for 15 minutes.
3. Add sliced tomatoes and bake for another 5 minutes or until golden and bubbly.
4. Top with fresh lettuce and a drizzle of mayo before serving.

Nutritional Information: 700 calories, 25g protein, 65g carbohydrates, 40g fat, 4g fiber, 50mg cholesterol, 1,300mg sodium, 450mg potassium.

Reuben Sandwich Pizza

Yield: 4 servings | Prep Time: 30 minutes | Cook Time: 20 minutes

Ingredients:

- Pizza dough
- Corned beef
- Sauerkraut
- Swiss cheese
- Thousand Island dressing
- Caraway seeds

Directions:

1. Preheat oven to 475°F (245°C).
2. Roll out the dough, add corned beef, sauerkraut, and Swiss cheese.
3. Bake for 20 minutes or until golden and bubbly.
4. Drizzle with Thousand Island dressing and sprinkle with caraway seeds before serving.

Nutritional Information: 740 calories, 35g protein, 70g carbohydrates, 35g fat, 5g fiber, 90mg cholesterol, 1,400mg sodium, 500mg potassium.

Cordon Bleu Pizza

Yield: 4 servings | Prep Time: 30 minutes | Cook Time: 20 minutes

Ingredients:

- Pizza dough
- Chicken breast
- Ham
- Swiss cheese
- Dijon mustard

Directions:

1. Preheat oven to 475°F (245°C).
2. Roll out the dough, add cooked chicken breast, ham, and Swiss cheese.
3. Bake for 20 minutes or until golden and bubbly.
4. Drizzle with Dijon mustard before serving.

Nutritional Information: 720 calories, 40g protein, 70g carbohydrates, 30g fat, 5g fiber, 90mg cholesterol, 1,200mg sodium, 500mg potassium.

Vietnamese Banh Mi Pizza

Yield: 4 servings | Prep Time: 30 minutes | Cook Time: 20 minutes

Ingredients:

- Pizza dough
- Grilled pork
- Pickled vegetables (carrots, daikon radish)
- Cilantro
- Jalapenos
- Sriracha mayo

Directions:

1. Preheat oven to 475°F (245°C).
2. Roll out the dough, add grilled pork and pickled vegetables.
3. Bake for 20 minutes or until golden and bubbly.
4. Top with fresh cilantro, jalapenos, and a drizzle of sriracha mayo before serving.

Nutritional Information: 700 calories, 30g protein, 70g carbohydrates, 30g fat, 5g fiber, 80mg cholesterol, 1,300mg sodium, 500mg potassium.

English Breakfast Pizza

Yield: 4 servings | Prep Time: 30 minutes | Cook Time: 20 minutes

Ingredients:

- Pizza dough
- Bacon
- Sausage
- Mushrooms
- Baked beans
- Eggs

Directions:

1. Preheat oven to 475°F (245°C).
2. Roll out the dough, add bacon, sausage, mushrooms, and baked beans.
3. Crack the eggs on top and bake for 20 minutes or until the eggs are cooked to your liking.

Nutritional Information: 780 calories, 40g protein, 70g carbohydrates, 40g fat, 5g fiber, 210mg cholesterol, 1,400mg sodium, 500mg potassium.

Chicken Souvlaki Pizza

Yield: 4 servings | Prep Time: 30 minutes | Cook Time: 20 minutes

Ingredients:

- Pizza dough
- Chicken breast
- Tomatoes
- Red onions
- Feta cheese
- Tzatziki sauce

Directions:

1. Preheat oven to 475°F (245°C).
2. Roll out the dough, add cooked chicken breast, tomatoes, red onions, and feta cheese.
3. Bake for 20 minutes or until golden and bubbly.
4. Drizzle with tzatziki sauce before serving.

Nutritional Information: 700 calories, 35g protein, 70g carbohydrates, 30g fat, 5g fiber, 80mg cholesterol, 1,200mg sodium, 500mg potassium.

Sausage and Gravy Breakfast Pizza

Yield: 4 servings | Prep Time: 20 minutes | Cook Time: 20 minutes

Ingredients:

- Pizza dough
- Breakfast sausage
- Gravy
- Eggs
- Cheddar cheese

Directions:

1. Preheat oven to 475°F (245°C).
2. Roll out the dough, add sausage, gravy, and crack the eggs on top.
3. Bake for 10 minutes, then sprinkle with cheese and bake for another 10 minutes until cheese is melted and bubbly.

Nutritional Information: 800 calories, 35g protein, 70g carbohydrates, 45g fat, 5g fiber, 230mg cholesterol, 1,300mg sodium, 500mg potassium.

Goat Cheese and Red Beet Pizza

Yield: 4 servings | Prep Time: 30 minutes | Cook Time: 20 minutes

Ingredients:

- Pizza dough
- Goat cheese
- Red beets, roasted and sliced
- Arugula
- Balsamic glaze

Directions:

1. Preheat oven to 475°F (245°C).
2. Roll out the dough, add goat cheese and beet slices.
3. Bake for 20 minutes or until golden and bubbly.
4. Top with arugula and a drizzle of balsamic glaze before serving.

Nutritional Information: 600 calories, 25g protein, 80g carbohydrates, 20g fat, 5g fiber, 45mg cholesterol, 1,000mg sodium, 600mg potassium.

Sausage, Peppers, and Onions Pizza

Yield: 4 servings | Prep Time: 20 minutes | Cook Time: 20 minutes

Ingredients:

- Pizza dough
- Italian sausage
- Bell peppers, sliced
- Onion, sliced
- Mozzarella cheese

Directions:

1. Preheat oven to 475°F (245°C).
2. Roll out the dough, add sausage, bell peppers, onions, and cheese.
3. Bake for 20 minutes or until golden and bubbly.

Nutritional Information: 750 calories, 30g protein, 70g carbohydrates, 40g fat, 5g fiber, 75mg cholesterol, 1,400mg sodium, 500mg potassium.

Chimichurri Steak Pizza

Yield: 4 servings | Prep Time: 40 minutes | Cook Time: 20 minutes

Ingredients:

- Pizza dough
- Steak, cooked and thinly sliced
- Chimichurri sauce
- Mozzarella cheese

Directions:

1. Preheat oven to 475°F (245°C).
2. Roll out the dough, add steak, chimichurri sauce, and cheese.
3. Bake for 20 minutes or until golden and bubbly.

Nutritional Information: 800 calories, 40g protein, 70g carbohydrates, 40g fat, 5g fiber, 90mg cholesterol, 1,300mg sodium, 500mg potassium.

Peking Duck Pizza

Yield: 4 servings | Prep Time: 40 minutes | Cook Time: 20 minutes

Ingredients:

- Pizza dough
- Duck breast, cooked and thinly sliced
- Hoisin sauce
- Green onions
- Cucumbers, thinly sliced

Directions:

1. Preheat oven to 475°F (245°C).
2. Roll out the dough, add duck slices and hoisin sauce.
3. Bake for 20 minutes or until golden and bubbly.
4. Top with green onions and cucumber slices before serving.

Nutritional Information: 800 calories, 35g protein, 70g carbohydrates, 40g fat, 5g fiber, 90mg cholesterol, 1,400mg sodium, 500mg potassium.

Apple, Walnut, and Blue Cheese Pizza

Yield: 4 servings | Prep time: 20 minutes | Cook time: 15 minutes

Ingredients:

- 1 pizza dough
- 1 cup blue cheese crumbles
- 1 large apple, thinly sliced
- 1/2 cup chopped walnuts
- 1 tablespoon olive oil
- 1 tablespoon honey
- 1/2 teaspoon ground cinnamon

Directions:

1. Preheat the oven to 450°F (230°C). Roll out the pizza dough on a floured surface to your desired thickness.
2. Spread the olive oil over the dough, then evenly distribute the blue cheese, apple slices, and chopped walnuts over the top.
3. Drizzle the honey and sprinkle the cinnamon over the toppings.
4. Bake in the preheated oven for 15 minutes or until the crust is golden and the cheese has melted.

Nutritional Information: 450 calories, 14g protein, 60g carbohydrates, 18g fat, 4g fiber, 30mg cholesterol, 800mg sodium, 200mg potassium.

Lemon, Smoked Salmon, and Dill Pizza

Yield: 2 servings | Prep time: 15 minutes | Cook time: 12 minutes

Ingredients:

- 1 pizza dough
- 1/2 cup cream cheese
- 1/2 lemon, zested and juiced
- 1 cup smoked salmon, thinly sliced
- 2 tablespoons fresh dill, chopped
- 1 tablespoon capers

Directions:

1. Preheat the oven to 450°F (230°C). Roll out the pizza dough on a floured surface to your desired thickness.
2. Spread the cream cheese over the dough, then evenly distribute the smoked salmon.
3. Sprinkle over the lemon zest, drizzle with lemon juice, then scatter over the capers and dill.
4. Bake in the preheated oven for 12 minutes or until the crust is golden.

Nutritional Information: 520 calories, 28g protein, 58g carbohydrates, 20g fat, 2g fiber, 50mg cholesterol, 960mg sodium, 220mg potassium.

Barbecue Jackfruit Pizza

Yield: 6 servings | Prep time: 25 minutes | Cook time: 20 minutes

Ingredients:

- 1 pizza dough
- 1 cup barbecue sauce
- 2 cups jackfruit, shredded
- 1/2 red onion, thinly sliced
- 1 bell pepper, thinly sliced
- 2 cups vegan mozzarella chees

Directions:

1. Preheat the oven to 450°F (230°C). Roll out the pizza dough on a floured surface to your desired thickness.
2. Spread the barbecue sauce over the dough, then evenly distribute the shredded jackfruit, sliced onion, and bell pepper.
3. Top with the vegan mozzarella cheese.
4. Bake in the preheated oven for 20 minutes or until the crust is golden and the cheese has melted.

Nutritional Information: 400 calories, 10g protein, 72g carbohydrates, 10g fat, 6g fiber, 0mg cholesterol, 790mg sodium, 240mg potassium.

Blue Cheese and Hot Honey Pizza

Yield: 4 servings | Prep time: 15 minutes | Cook time: 15 minutes

Ingredients:

- 1 pizza dough
- 1 cup blue cheese crumbles
- 1/2 cup hot honey
- 1 tablespoon olive oil
- 1/2 cup walnuts, roughly chopped

Directions:

1. Preheat the oven to 450°F (230°C). Roll out the pizza dough on a floured surface to your desired thickness.
2. Spread the olive oil over the dough, then evenly distribute the blue cheese and walnuts.
3. Drizzle the hot honey over the toppings.
4. Bake in the preheated oven for 15 minutes or until the crust is golden and the cheese has melted.

Nutritional Information: 520 calories, 14g protein, 66g carbohydrates, 24g fat, 3g fiber, 30mg cholesterol, 860mg sodium, 180mg potassium.

Pastrami and Pickles Pizza

Yield: 4 servings | Prep time: 20 minutes | Cook time: 18 minutes

Ingredients:

- 1 pizza dough
- 1/2 cup pizza sauce
- 2 cups shredded mozzarella cheese
- 1 cup pastrami, chopped
- 1/2 cup pickles, thinly sliced

Directions:

1. Preheat the oven to 450°F (230°C). Roll out the pizza dough on a floured surface to your desired thickness.
2. Spread the pizza sauce over the dough, then evenly distribute the mozzarella cheese and pastrami.
3. Arrange the sliced pickles over the toppings.
4. Bake in the preheated oven for 18 minutes or until the crust is golden and the cheese has melted.

Nutritional Information: 580 calories, 32g protein, 58g carbohydrates, 26g fat, 2g fiber, 70mg cholesterol, 1260mg sodium, 250mg potassium.

Shrimp and Grits Pizza

Yield: 4 servings | Prep time: 20 minutes | Cook time: 20 minutes

Ingredients:

- 1 pizza dough
- 1 cup grits, cooked
- 1 cup cheddar cheese, shredded
- 1 lb shrimp, peeled and deveined
- 1/2 teaspoon Cajun seasoning
- 2 tablespoons olive oil

Directions:

1. Preheat the oven to 450°F (230°C). Roll out the pizza dough on a floured surface to your desired thickness.
2. Spread the cooked grits over the dough, then evenly distribute the shredded cheddar cheese.
3. Toss the shrimp with the Cajun seasoning and arrange them on the pizza.
4. Drizzle with olive oil.
5. Bake in the preheated oven for 20 minutes or until the crust is golden and the cheese has melted.

Nutritional Information: 500 calories, 30g protein, 58g carbohydrates, 18g fat, 3g fiber, 190mg cholesterol, 1000mg sodium, 200mg potassium.

Pulled Pork and Coleslaw Pizza

Yield: 6 servings | Prep time: 25 minutes | Cook time: 20 minutes

Ingredients:

- 1 pizza dough
- 2 cups pulled pork
- 1 cup barbecue sauce
- 1 cup coleslaw
- 2 cups mozzarella cheese, shredded

Directions:

1. Preheat the oven to 450°F (230°C). Roll out the pizza dough on a floured surface to your desired thickness.
2. Spread the barbecue sauce over the dough, then evenly distribute the pulled pork.
3. Top with the shredded mozzarella cheese.
4. Bake in the preheated oven for 20 minutes or until the crust is golden and the cheese has melted.
5. Remove from the oven and top with coleslaw before serving.

Nutritional Information: 650 calories, 32g protein, 72g carbohydrates, 28g fat, 4g fiber, 85mg cholesterol, 1400mg sodium, 300mg potassium.

Curry Chicken Pizza

Yield: 4 servings | Prep time: 25 minutes | Cook time: 20 minutes

Ingredients:

- 1 pizza dough
- 1 cup cooked chicken, diced
- 1/2 cup curry sauce
- 1 red bell pepper, thinly sliced
- 2 cups mozzarella cheese, shredded

Directions:

1. Preheat the oven to 450°F (230°C). Roll out the pizza dough on a floured surface to your desired thickness.
2. Spread the curry sauce over the dough, then evenly distribute the diced chicken and sliced bell pepper.
3. Top with the shredded mozzarella cheese.
4. Bake in the preheated oven for 20 minutes or until the crust is golden and the cheese has melted.

Nutritional Information: 520 calories, 30g protein, 60g carbohydrates, 20g fat, 3g fiber, 65mg cholesterol, 900mg sodium, 240mg potassium.

Chicken, Bacon, Ranch Pizza

Yield: 4 servings | Prep time: 20 minutes | Cook time: 20 minutes

Ingredients:

- 1 pizza dough
- 1 cup cooked chicken, diced
- 1/2 cup ranch dressing
- 1/2 cup bacon, cooked and crumbled
- 2 cups mozzarella cheese, shredded

Directions:

1. Preheat the oven to 450°F (230°C). Roll out the pizza dough on a floured surface to your desired thickness.
2. Spread the ranch dressing over the dough, then evenly distribute the diced chicken and crumbled bacon.
3. Top with the shredded mozzarella cheese.
4. Bake in the preheated oven for 20 minutes or until the crust is golden and the cheese has melted.

Nutritional Information: 620 calories, 32g protein, 58g carbohydrates, 30g fat, 2g fiber, 90mg cholesterol, 1200mg sodium, 250mg potassium.

Garlic, Spinach, and Chicken Pizza

Yield: 4 servings | Prep time: 20 minutes | Cook time: 20 minutes

Ingredients:

- 1 pizza dough
- 1 cup cooked chicken, diced
- 2 cloves garlic, minced
- 1 cup fresh spinach leaves
- 2 cups mozzarella cheese, shredded
- 1 tablespoon olive oil

Directions:

1. Preheat the oven to 450°F (230°C). Roll out the pizza dough on a floured surface to your desired thickness.
2. Spread the olive oil over the dough, then sprinkle over the minced garlic.
3. Distribute the diced chicken and spinach leaves evenly over the pizza.
4. Top with the shredded mozzarella cheese.
5. Bake in the preheated oven for 20 minutes or until the crust is golden and the cheese has melted.

Nutritional Information: 520 calories, 30g protein, 60g carbohydrates, 20g fat, 3g fiber, 65mg cholesterol, 900mg sodium, 240mg potassium.

Hawaiian BBQ Chicken Pizza

Yield: 4 servings | Prep time: 20 minutes | Cook time: 20 minutes

Ingredients:

- 1 pizza dough
- 1 cup barbecue sauce
- 1 cup cooked chicken, diced
- 1 cup pineapple chunks
- 1 cup mozzarella cheese, shredded
- 1/2 cup red onion, thinly sliced

Directions:

1. Preheat the oven to 450°F (230°C). Roll out the pizza dough on a floured surface to your desired thickness.
2. Spread the barbecue sauce over the dough, then evenly distribute the diced chicken, pineapple chunks, and red onion.
3. Top with the shredded mozzarella cheese.
4. Bake in the preheated oven for 20 minutes or until the crust is golden and the cheese has melted.

Nutritional Information: 520 calories, 25g protein, 75g carbohydrates, 16g fat, 4g fiber, 60mg cholesterol, 1020mg sodium, 280mg potassium.

Tomato, Basil, and Mozzarella Pizza

Yield: 2 servings | Prep time: 15 minutes | Cook time: 12 minutes

Ingredients:

- 1 pizza dough
- 1 cup mozzarella cheese, shredded
- 2 large tomatoes, thinly sliced
- 1/4 cup fresh basil leaves
- 1 tablespoon olive oil
- Salt and pepper to taste

Directions:

1. Preheat the oven to 450°F (230°C). Roll out the pizza dough on a floured surface to your desired thickness.
2. Spread the olive oil over the dough, then evenly distribute the sliced tomatoes and shredded mozzarella.
3. Season with salt and pepper.
4. Bake in the preheated oven for 12 minutes or until the crust is golden and the cheese has melted.
5. Remove from the oven and top with fresh basil leaves before serving.

Nutritional Information: 480 calories, 20g protein, 60g carbohydrates, 18g fat, 3g fiber, 45mg cholesterol, 940mg sodium, 250mg potassium.

Philly Cheesesteak Pizza

Yield: 4 servings | Prep time: 20 minutes | Cook time: 20 minutes

Ingredients:

- 1 pizza dough
- 1/2 lb thinly sliced steak
- 1/2 onion, thinly sliced
- 1/2 green bell pepper, thinly sliced
- 2 cups provolone cheese, shredded
- 1 tablespoon olive oil
- Salt and pepper to taste

Directions:

1. Preheat the oven to 450°F (230°C). Roll out the pizza dough on a floured surface to your desired thickness.
2. Spread the olive oil over the dough, then evenly distribute the sliced steak, onion, and bell pepper.
3. Season with salt and pepper, then top with the shredded provolone cheese.
4. Bake in the preheated oven for 20 minutes or until the crust is golden and the cheese has melted.

Nutritional Information: 580 calories, 32g protein, 60g carbohydrates, 26g fat, 2g fiber, 70mg cholesterol, 1260mg sodium, 250mg potassium.

Baked Ziti Pizza

Yield: 6 servings | Prep time: 25 minutes | Cook time: 25 minutes

Ingredients:

- 1 pizza dough
- 2 cups ziti pasta, cooked
- 1 cup marinara sauce
- 2 cups mozzarella cheese, shredded
- 1/2 cup parmesan cheese, grated
- 1 tablespoon olive oil

Directions:

1. Preheat the oven to 450°F (230°C). Roll out the pizza dough on a floured surface to your desired thickness.
2. Spread the marinara sauce over the dough, then evenly distribute the cooked ziti.
3. Top with the shredded mozzarella and grated parmesan cheeses.
4. Drizzle with olive oil.
5. Bake in the preheated oven for 25 minutes or until the crust is golden and the cheese has melted.

Nutritional Information: 620 calories, 28g protein, 82g carbohydrates, 20g fat, 4g fiber, 45mg cholesterol, 1040mg sodium, 320mg potassium.

Guacamole and Shrimp Pizza

Yield: 4 servings | Prep time: 20 minutes | Cook time: 20 minutes

Ingredients:

- 1 pizza dough
- 1 cup guacamole
- 1 lb shrimp, peeled and deveined
- 1/2 cup red onion, thinly sliced
- 2 cups mozzarella cheese, shredded
- 1/2 cup fresh cilantro leaves

Directions:

1. Preheat the oven to 450°F (230°C). Roll out the pizza dough on a floured surface to your desired thickness.
2. Spread the guacamole over the dough, then evenly distribute the shrimp and red onion.
3. Top with the shredded mozzarella cheese.
4. Bake in the preheated oven for 20 minutes or until the crust is golden and the cheese has melted.
5. Remove from the oven and top with fresh cilantro leaves before serving.

Nutritional Information: 530 calories, 35g protein, 60g carbohydrates, 18g fat, 4g fiber, 190mg cholesterol, 990mg sodium, 300mg potassium.

Taco Supreme Pizza

Yield: 4 servings | Prep time: 25 minutes | Cook time: 15 minutes

Ingredients:

- 1 pizza dough
- 1 cup taco sauce
- 1 cup ground beef, cooked and seasoned with taco seasoning
- 1 cup cheddar cheese, shredded
- 1/2 cup tomatoes, diced
- 1/4 cup black olives, sliced
- 1/4 cup green onions, chopped
- 1/2 cup sour cream

Directions:

1. Preheat the oven to 450°F (230°C). Roll out the pizza dough on a floured surface to your desired thickness.
2. Spread the taco sauce over the dough, then evenly distribute the cooked beef.
3. Top with the shredded cheddar cheese, diced tomatoes, and sliced olives.
4. Bake in the preheated oven for 15 minutes or until the crust is golden and the cheese has melted.
5. Remove from the oven and top with chopped green onions and dollops of sour cream before serving.

Nutritional Information: 560 calories, 28g protein, 62g carbohydrates, 22g fat, 3g fiber, 70mg cholesterol, 1180mg sodium, 320mg potassium.

Chicken Quesadilla Pizza

Yield: 4 servings | Prep time: 20 minutes | Cook time: 15 minutes

Ingredients:

- 1 pizza dough
- 1 cup salsa
- 1 cup cooked chicken, diced
- 1 cup Monterey Jack cheese, shredded
- 1/2 cup bell peppers, thinly sliced
- 1/2 cup onions, thinly sliced
- 1/4 cup fresh cilantro, chopped

Directions:

1. Preheat the oven to 450°F (230°C). Roll out the pizza dough on a floured surface to your desired thickness.
2. Spread the salsa over the dough, then evenly distribute the diced chicken, sliced peppers, and onions.
3. Top with the shredded Monterey Jack cheese.
4. Bake in the preheated oven for 15 minutes or until the crust is golden and the cheese has melted.
5. Remove from the oven and top with chopped cilantro before serving.

Nutritional Information: 490 calories, 26g protein, 58g carbohydrates, 18g fat, 3g fiber, 65mg cholesterol, 1050mg sodium, 280mg potassium.

Pad Thai Pizza

Yield: 2 servings | Prep time: 30 minutes | Cook time: 15 minutes

Ingredients:

- 1 pizza dough
- 1 cup cooked shrimp
- 1/2 cup bean sprouts
- 1/2 cup carrots, julienned
- 1/4 cup green onions, chopped
- 1/4 cup peanuts, crushed
- 1/2 cup Pad Thai sauce
- 1 cup mozzarella cheese, shredded

Directions:

1. Preheat the oven to 450°F (230°C). Roll out the pizza dough on a floured surface to your desired thickness.
2. Spread the Pad Thai sauce over the dough, then evenly distribute the cooked shrimp, bean sprouts, and carrots.
3. Top with the shredded mozzarella cheese.
4. Bake in the preheated oven for 15 minutes or until the crust is golden and the cheese has melted.
5. Remove from the oven and top with chopped green onions and crushed peanuts before serving.

Nutritional Information: 540 calories, 28g protein, 64g carbohydrates, 20g fat, 4g fiber, 165mg cholesterol, 1150mg sodium, 340mg potassium.

Pulled Pork and Pineapple Pizza

Yield: 4 servings | Prep time: 20 minutes | Cook time: 15 minutes

Ingredients:

- 1 pizza dough
- 1 cup barbecue sauce
- 1 cup pulled pork
- 1 cup pineapple chunks
- 1 cup mozzarella cheese, shredded
- 1/2 cup red onion, thinly sliced

Directions:

1. Preheat the oven to 450°F (230°C). Roll out the pizza dough on a floured surface to your desired thickness.
2. Spread the barbecue sauce over the dough, then evenly distribute the pulled pork, pineapple chunks, and red onion.
3. Top with the shredded mozzarella cheese.
4. Bake in the preheated oven for 15 minutes or until the crust is golden and the cheese has melted.

Nutritional Information: 560 calories, 25g protein, 74g carbohydrates, 20g fat, 3g fiber, 70mg cholesterol, 1130mg sodium, 320mg potassium.

Fennel Sausage and Pepper Pizza

Yield: 4 servings | Prep time: 20 minutes | Cook time: 20 minutes

Ingredients:

- 1 pizza dough
- 1 cup fennel sausage, cooked and crumbled
- 1/2 cup bell peppers, thinly sliced
- 1/2 cup onion, thinly sliced
- 2 cups mozzarella cheese, shredded
- 1 tablespoon olive oil

Directions:

1. Preheat the oven to 450°F (230°C). Roll out the pizza dough on a floured surface to your desired thickness.
2. Spread the olive oil over the dough, then evenly distribute the cooked sausage, sliced peppers, and onions.
3. Top with the shredded mozzarella cheese.
4. Bake in the preheated oven for 20 minutes or until the crust is golden and the cheese has melted.

Nutritional Information: 590 calories, 26g protein, 62g carbohydrates, 26g fat, 2g fiber, 65mg cholesterol, 1220mg sodium, 300mg potassium.

Teriyaki Chicken and Pineapple Pizza

Yield: 4 servings | Prep time: 25 minutes | Cook time: 15 minutes

Ingredients:

- 1 pizza dough
- 1 cup teriyaki sauce
- 1 cup cooked chicken, diced
- 1 cup pineapple chunks
- 1/2 cup red onions, thinly sliced
- 2 cups mozzarella cheese, shredded

Directions:

1. Preheat the oven to 450°F (230°C). Roll out the pizza dough on a floured surface to your desired thickness.
2. Spread the teriyaki sauce over the dough, then evenly distribute the diced chicken, pineapple chunks, and sliced red onions.
3. Top with the shredded mozzarella cheese.
4. Bake in the preheated oven for 15 minutes or until the crust is golden and the cheese has melted.

Nutritional Information: 580 calories, 30g protein, 72g carbohydrates, 20g fat, 2g fiber, 80mg cholesterol, 2100mg sodium, 400mg potassium.

Margherita with Balsamic Reduction Pizza

Yield: 2 servings | Prep time: 15 minutes | Cook time: 15 minutes

Ingredients:

- 1 pizza dough
- 1 cup fresh tomatoes, sliced
- 1 cup fresh mozzarella cheese, sliced
- Fresh basil leaves
- 1/2 cup balsamic reduction
- 2 tablespoons olive oil

Directions:

1. Preheat the oven to 450°F (230°C). Roll out the pizza dough on a floured surface to your desired thickness.
2. Drizzle the olive oil over the dough, arrange the sliced tomatoes and mozzarella evenly on the dough.
3. Bake in the preheated oven for 15 minutes or until the crust is golden and the cheese has melted.
4. Remove from the oven, garnish with fresh basil leaves, and drizzle with balsamic reduction before serving.

Nutritional Information: 550 calories, 20g protein, 68g carbohydrates, 23g fat, 3g fiber, 45mg cholesterol, 680mg sodium, 300mg potassium.

Shrimp, Lobster, and Crab Pizza

Yield: 4 servings | Prep time: 30 minutes | Cook time: 20 minutes

Ingredients:

- 1 pizza dough
- 1 cup marinara sauce
- 1/2 cup cooked shrimp, peeled and deveined
- 1/2 cup cooked lobster meat
- 1/2 cup cooked crab meat
- 2 cups mozzarella cheese, shredded
- 1/4 cup parsley, chopped

Directions:

1. Preheat the oven to 450°F (230°C). Roll out the pizza dough on a floured surface to your desired thickness.
2. Spread the marinara sauce over the dough, then evenly distribute the shrimp, lobster, and crab.
3. Top with the shredded mozzarella cheese.
4. Bake in the preheated oven for 20 minutes or until the crust is golden and the cheese has melted.
5. Remove from the oven and sprinkle with chopped parsley before serving.

Nutritional Information: 600 calories, 40g protein, 66g carbohydrates, 20g fat, 4g fiber, 175mg cholesterol, 1700mg sodium, 400mg potassium.

Portobello and Spinach Pizza

Yield: 2 servings | Prep time: 20 minutes | Cook time: 15 minutes

Ingredients:

- 1 pizza dough
- 1 cup portobello mushrooms, sliced
- 1 cup fresh spinach
- 2 cups mozzarella cheese, shredded
- 2 tablespoons olive oil
- 1/2 cup cherry tomatoes, halved
- Salt and pepper to taste

Directions:

1. Preheat the oven to 450°F (230°C). Roll out the pizza dough on a floured surface to your desired thickness.
2. Drizzle the olive oil over the dough, arrange the sliced mushrooms and spinach evenly on the dough. Season with salt and pepper.
3. Top with the shredded mozzarella cheese and cherry tomatoes.
4. Bake in the preheated oven for 15 minutes or until the crust is golden and the cheese has melted.

Nutritional Information: 530 calories, 24g protein, 60g carbohydrates, 23g fat, 4g fiber, 45mg cholesterol, 720mg sodium, 350mg potassium.

Chicken Parmesan Pizza

Yield: 4 servings | Prep time: 25 minutes | Cook time: 20 minutes

Ingredients:

- 1 pizza dough
- 1 cup marinara sauce
- 1 cup cooked chicken, diced
- 2 cups mozzarella cheese, shredded
- 1/2 cup parmesan cheese, grated
- 1 tablespoon olive oil

Directions:

1. Preheat the oven to 450°F (230°C). Roll out the pizza dough on a floured surface to your desired thickness.
2. Spread the marinara sauce over the dough, then evenly distribute the diced chicken.
3. Top with the shredded mozzarella cheese and grated parmesan cheese.
4. Drizzle with olive oil.
5. Bake in the preheated oven for 20 minutes or until the crust is golden and the cheese has melted.

Nutritional Information: 570 calories, 30g protein, 66g carbohydrates, 23g fat, 3g fiber, 70mg cholesterol, 1370mg sodium, 380mg potassium.

Provolone and Pepperoni Pizza

Yield: 4 servings | Prep time: 15 minutes | Cook time: 15 minutes

Ingredients:

- 1 pizza dough
- 1 cup pizza sauce
- 2 cups provolone cheese, shredded
- 1 cup pepperoni slices

Directions:

1. Preheat the oven to 450°F (230°C). Roll out the pizza dough on a floured surface to your desired thickness.
2. Spread the pizza sauce over the dough, then evenly distribute the pepperoni slices.
3. Top with the shredded provolone cheese.
4. Bake in the preheated oven for 15 minutes or until the crust is golden and the cheese has melted.

Nutritional Information: 610 calories, 30g protein, 68g carbohydrates, 26g fat, 4g fiber, 65mg cholesterol, 1400mg sodium, 370mg potassium.

Pesto, Mozzarella, and Tomato Pizza

Yield: 2 servings | Prep time: 15 minutes | Cook time: 15 minutes

Ingredients:

- 1 pizza dough
- 1/2 cup pesto sauce
- 1 cup fresh mozzarella cheese, sliced
- 1 cup fresh tomatoes, sliced

Directions:

1. Preheat the oven to 450°F (230°C). Roll out the pizza dough on a floured surface to your desired thickness.
2. Spread the pesto sauce over the dough, then evenly distribute the sliced tomatoes.
3. Top with the sliced mozzarella cheese.
4. Bake in the preheated oven for 15 minutes or until the crust is golden and the cheese has melted.

Nutritional Information: 510 calories, 22g protein, 66g carbohydrates, 20g fat, 3g fiber, 45mg cholesterol, 840mg sodium, 310mg potassium.

Alfredo, Chicken, and Broccoli Pizza

Yield: 4 servings | Prep time: 20 minutes | Cook time: 20 minutes

Ingredients:

- 1 pizza dough
- 1 cup Alfredo sauce
- 1 cup cooked chicken, diced
- 1 cup broccoli florets
- 2 cups mozzarella cheese, shredded

Directions:

1. Preheat the oven to 450°F (230°C). Roll out the pizza dough on a floured surface to your desired thickness.
2. Spread the Alfredo sauce over the dough, then evenly distribute the diced chicken and broccoli florets.
3. Top with the shredded mozzarella cheese.
4. Bake in the preheated oven for 20 minutes or until the crust is golden and the cheese has melted.

Nutritional Information: 590 calories, 32g protein, 68g carbohydrates, 23g fat, 3g fiber, 85mg cholesterol, 1250mg sodium, 400mg potassium.

Ricotta, Mozzarella, and Basil Pizza

Yield: 2 servings | Prep time: 15 minutes | Cook time: 15 minutes

Ingredients:

- 1 pizza dough
- 1/2 cup ricotta cheese
- 1 cup mozzarella cheese, shredded
- Fresh basil leaves

Directions:

1. Preheat the oven to 450°F (230°C). Roll out the pizza dough on a floured surface to your desired thickness.
2. Spread the ricotta cheese over the dough, then evenly distribute the shredded mozzarella.
3. Bake in the preheated oven for 15 minutes or until the crust is golden and the cheese has melted.
4. Remove from the oven and garnish with fresh basil leaves before serving.

Nutritional Information: 540 calories, 26g protein, 66g carbohydrates, 22g fat, 3g fiber, 60mg cholesterol, 710mg sodium, 300mg potassium.

Goat Cheese and Spinach Pizza

Yield: 2 servings | Prep time: 15 minutes | Cook time: 15 minutes

Ingredients:

- 1 pizza dough
- 1 cup goat cheese, crumbled
- 2 cups fresh spinach
- 2 tablespoons olive oil
- Salt and pepper to taste

Directions:

1. Preheat the oven to 450°F (230°C). Roll out the pizza dough on a floured surface to your desired thickness.
2. Drizzle the olive oil over the dough, arrange the fresh spinach evenly on the dough. Season with salt and pepper.
3. Top with the crumbled goat cheese.
4. Bake in the preheated oven for 15 minutes or until the crust is golden and the cheese has melted.

Nutritional Information: 510 calories, 18g protein, 66g carbohydrates, 22g fat, 3g fiber, 45mg cholesterol, 680mg sodium, 300mg potassium.

Egg, Bacon, and Spinach Breakfast Pizza

Yield: 4 servings | Prep time: 20 minutes | Cook time: 15 minutes

Ingredients:

- 1 pizza dough
- 4 large eggs
- 6 slices bacon, cooked and crumbled
- 2 cups spinach
- 1 cup cheddar cheese, shredded
- 1 tablespoon olive oil
- Salt and pepper to taste

Directions:

1. Preheat the oven to 450°F (230°C). Roll out the pizza dough on a floured surface to your desired thickness.
2. Drizzle the olive oil over the dough, arrange the spinach and crumbled bacon evenly on the dough. Season with salt and pepper.
3. Make wells in the toppings and crack an egg into each well.
4. Sprinkle with the shredded cheddar cheese.
5. Bake in the preheated oven for 15 minutes or until the crust is golden, the cheese has melted, and the eggs are cooked to your liking.

Nutritional Information: 550 calories, 28g protein, 66g carbohydrates, 23g fat, 4g fiber, 215mg cholesterol, 1030mg sodium, 400mg potassium.

Pancetta, Arugula, and Tomato Pizza

Yield: 2 servings | Prep time: 15 minutes | Cook time: 15 minutes

Ingredients:

- 1 pizza dough
- 1/2 cup pancetta, diced
- 2 cups arugula
- 1 cup cherry tomatoes, halved
- 1 cup mozzarella cheese, shredded
- 1 tablespoon olive oil

Directions:

1. Preheat the oven to 450°F (230°C). Roll out the pizza dough on a floured surface to your desired thickness.
2. Drizzle the olive oil over the dough, arrange the pancetta and cherry tomatoes evenly on the dough.
3. Sprinkle with the shredded mozzarella cheese.
4. Bake in the preheated oven for 15 minutes or until the crust is golden and the cheese has melted.
5. Remove from the oven and top with the fresh arugula before serving.

Nutritional Information: 520 calories, 24g protein, 66g carbohydrates, 22g fat, 3g fiber, 50mg cholesterol, 950mg sodium, 350mg potassium.

Eggplant, Tomato, and Pesto Pizza

Yield: 4 servings | Prep time: 20 minutes | Cook time: 20 minutes

Ingredients:

- 1 pizza dough
- 1/2 cup pesto sauce
- 1 small eggplant, thinly sliced
- 1 cup cherry tomatoes, halved
- 2 cups mozzarella cheese, shredded

Directions:

1. Preheat the oven to 450°F (230°C). Roll out the pizza dough on a floured surface to your desired thickness.
2. Spread the pesto sauce over the dough, then arrange the sliced eggplant and halved tomatoes evenly on the dough.
3. Sprinkle with the shredded mozzarella cheese.
4. Bake in the preheated oven for 20 minutes or until the crust is golden and the cheese has melted.

Nutritional Information: 570 calories, 24g protein, 68g carbohydrates, 24g fat, 5g fiber, 45mg cholesterol, 840mg sodium, 520mg potassium.

Butternut Squash and Caramelized Onion Pizza

Yield: 4 servings | Prep time: 30 minutes | Cook time: 20 minutes

Ingredients:

- 1 pizza dough
- 1 cup butternut squash, diced
- 1 large onion, sliced and caramelized
- 2 cups mozzarella cheese, shredded
- 1 tablespoon olive oil
- Salt and pepper to taste

Directions:

1. Preheat the oven to 450°F (230°C). Roll out the pizza dough on a floured surface to your desired thickness.
2. Drizzle the olive oil over the dough, arrange the caramelized onion and diced butternut squash evenly on the dough. Season with salt and pepper.
3. Sprinkle with the shredded mozzarella cheese.
4. Bake in the preheated oven for 20 minutes or until the crust is golden and the cheese has melted.

Nutritional Information: 540 calories, 22g protein, 72g carbohydrates, 20g fat, 5g fiber, 45mg cholesterol, 840mg sodium, 600mg potassium.

Vegan Margherita Pizza

Yield: 2 servings | Prep time: 15 minutes | Cook time: 15 minutes

Ingredients:

- 1 pizza dough
- 1/2 cup pizza sauce
- 1 cup vegan mozzarella cheese
- Fresh basil leaves
- 1 cup cherry tomatoes, halved

Directions:

1. Preheat the oven to 450°F (230°C). Roll out the pizza dough on a floured surface to your desired thickness.
2. Spread the pizza sauce over the dough, then arrange the halved tomatoes evenly on the dough.
3. Sprinkle with the vegan mozzarella cheese.
4. Bake in the preheated oven for 15 minutes or until the crust is golden and the cheese has melted.
5. Remove from the oven and garnish with fresh basil leaves before serving.

Nutritional Information: 490 calories, 12g protein, 82g carbohydrates, 12g fat, 5g fiber, 0mg cholesterol, 1040mg sodium, 380mg potassium.

Gluten-Free Pepperoni Pizza

Yield: 2 servings | Prep time: 10 minutes | Cook time: 15 minutes

Ingredients:

- 1 gluten-free pizza crust
- 1/2 cup pizza sauce
- 1 cup shredded mozzarella cheese
- 1/2 cup pepperoni slices

Directions:

1. Preheat the oven to 450°F (230°C). Place the gluten-free pizza crust on a baking sheet.
2. Spread the pizza sauce over the crust, then arrange the pepperoni slices evenly on the sauce.
3. Sprinkle with the shredded mozzarella cheese.
4. Bake in the preheated oven for 15 minutes or until the crust is crispy and the cheese has melted.

Nutritional Information: 530 calories, 23g protein, 46g carbohydrates, 29g fat, 2g fiber, 70mg cholesterol, 1300mg sodium, 350mg potassium.

Vegetarian Supreme Pizza

Yield: 4 servings | Prep time: 15 minutes | Cook time: 15 minutes

Ingredients:

- 1 pizza dough
- 1/2 cup pizza sauce
- 1 cup shredded mozzarella cheese
- 1/2 bell pepper, sliced
- 1/2 onion, sliced
- 1/2 cup mushrooms, sliced
- 1/2 cup black olives, sliced

Directions:

1. Preheat the oven to 450°F (230°C). Roll out the pizza dough on a floured surface to your desired thickness.
2. Spread the pizza sauce over the dough, then arrange the bell pepper, onion, mushrooms, and olives evenly on the sauce.
3. Sprinkle with the shredded mozzarella cheese.
4. Bake in the preheated oven for 15 minutes or until the crust is golden and the cheese has melted.

Nutritional Information: 480 calories, 20g protein, 70g carbohydrates, 15g fat, 4g fiber, 45mg cholesterol, 830mg sodium, 450mg potassium.

Vegan BBQ Jackfruit Pizza

Yield: 4 servings | Prep time: 20 minutes | Cook time: 20 minutes

Ingredients:

- 1 pizza dough
- 1/2 cup BBQ sauce
- 1 can jackfruit, drained and shredded
- 1/2 red onion, thinly sliced
- 1 cup vegan mozzarella cheese

Directions:

1. Preheat the oven to 450°F (230°C). Roll out the pizza dough on a floured surface to your desired thickness.
2. Spread the BBQ sauce over the dough, then arrange the shredded jackfruit and red onion evenly on the sauce.
3. Sprinkle with the vegan mozzarella cheese.
4. Bake in the preheated oven for 20 minutes or until the crust is golden and the cheese has melted.

Nutritional Information: 520 calories, 10g protein, 88g carbohydrates, 14g fat, 5g fiber, 0mg cholesterol, 1200mg sodium, 400mg potassium.

Gluten-Free Veggie Pizza

Yield: 2 servings | Prep time: 15 minutes | Cook time: 15 minutes

Ingredients:

- 1 gluten-free pizza crust
- 1/2 cup pizza sauce
- 1 cup shredded mozzarella cheese
- 1/2 bell pepper, sliced
- 1/2 onion, sliced
- 1/2 cup mushrooms, sliced

Directions:

1. Preheat the oven to 450°F (230°C). Place the gluten-free pizza crust on a baking sheet.
2. Spread the pizza sauce over the crust, then arrange the bell pepper, onion, and mushrooms evenly on the sauce.
3. Sprinkle with the shredded mozzarella cheese.
4. Bake in the preheated oven for 15 minutes or until the crust is crispy and the cheese has melted.

Nutritional Information: 460 calories, 18g protein, 52g carbohydrates, 22g fat, 3g fiber, 45mg cholesterol, 910mg sodium, 300mg potassium.

Keto Chicken and Spinach Pizza

Yield: 2 servings | Prep time: 10 minutes | Cook time: 20 minutes

Ingredients:

- 1 keto pizza crust
- 1/2 cup alfredo sauce
- 1 cup shredded mozzarella cheese
- 1 cup cooked chicken breast, diced
- 1 cup fresh spinach

Directions:

1. Preheat the oven to 450°F (230°C). Place the keto pizza crust on a baking sheet.
2. Spread the alfredo sauce over the crust, then arrange the diced chicken and spinach evenly on the sauce.
3. Sprinkle with the shredded mozzarella cheese.
4. Bake in the preheated oven for 20 minutes or until the crust is golden and the cheese has melted.

Nutritional Information: 550 calories, 42g protein, 8g carbohydrates, 40g fat, 3g fiber, 125mg cholesterol, 750mg sodium, 350mg potassium.

Vegan Roasted Vegetable Pizza

Yield: 4 servings | Prep time: 20 minutes | Cook time: 25 minutes

Ingredients:

- \- 1 pizza dough
- \- 1/2 cup pizza sauce
- \- 1 cup vegan mozzarella cheese
- \- 1 bell pepper, sliced
- \- 1 zucchini, sliced
- \- 1 red onion, sliced
- \- 1 cup cherry tomatoes

Directions:

1. Preheat the oven to 450°F (230°C). Roll out the pizza dough on a floured surface to your desired thickness.
2. Spread the pizza sauce over the dough, then arrange the bell pepper, zucchini, onion, and tomatoes evenly on the sauce.
3. Sprinkle with the vegan mozzarella cheese.
4. Bake in the preheated oven for 25 minutes or until the crust is golden and the cheese has melted.

Nutritional Information: 480 calories, 15g protein, 84g carbohydrates, 12g fat, 6g fiber, 0mg cholesterol, 950mg sodium, 520mg potassium.

Keto Meat Lover's Pizza

Yield: 2 servings | Prep time: 10 minutes | Cook time: 20 minutes

Ingredients:

- 1 keto pizza crust
- 1/2 cup pizza sauce
- 1 cup shredded mozzarella cheese
- 1/2 cup pepperoni slices
- 1/2 cup cooked sausage
- 1/2 cup cooked bacon

Directions:

1. Preheat the oven to 450°F (230°C). Place the keto pizza crust on a baking sheet.
2. Spread the pizza sauce over the crust, then arrange the pepperoni, sausage, and bacon evenly on the sauce.
3. Sprinkle with the shredded mozzarella cheese.
4. Bake in the preheated oven for 20 minutes or until the crust is golden and the cheese has melted.

Nutritional Information: 680 calories, 50g protein, 10g carbohydrates, 50g fat, 3g fiber, 120mg cholesterol, 1450mg sodium, 400mg potassium.

Vegan Mushroom and Bell Pepper Pizza

Yield: 4 servings | Prep time: 15 minutes | Cook time: 20 minutes

Ingredients:

- 1 pizza dough
- 1/2 cup pizza sauce
- 1 cup vegan mozzarella cheese
- 1 cup mushrooms, sliced
- 1 bell pepper, sliced

Directions:

1. Preheat the oven to 450°F (230°C). Roll out the pizza dough on a floured surface to your desired thickness.
2. Spread the pizza sauce over the dough, then arrange the mushrooms and bell pepper evenly on the sauce.
3. Sprinkle with the vegan mozzarella cheese.
4. Bake in the preheated oven for 20 minutes or until the crust is golden and the cheese has melted.

Nutritional Information: 470 calories, 15g protein, 82g carbohydrates, 12g fat, 5g fiber, 0mg cholesterol, 900mg sodium, 520mg potassium.

Gluten-Free Hawaiian Pizza

Yield: 2 servings | Prep time: 10 minutes | Cook time: 15 minutes

Ingredients:

- 1 gluten-free pizza crust
- 1/2 cup pizza sauce
- 1 cup shredded mozzarella cheese
- 1/2 cup ham, diced
- 1/2 cup pineapple chunks

Directions:

1. Preheat the oven to 450°F (230°C). Place the gluten-free pizza crust on a baking sheet.
2. Spread the pizza sauce over the crust, then arrange the ham and pineapple evenly on the sauce.
3. Sprinkle with the shredded mozzarella cheese.
4. Bake in the preheated oven for 15 minutes or until the crust is crispy and the cheese has melted.

Nutritional Information: 560 calories, 24g protein, 60g carbohydrates, 28g fat, 2g fiber, 70mg cholesterol, 1340mg sodium, 350mg potassium.

Keto Pepperoni and Cheese Pizza

Yield: 2 servings | Prep time: 10 minutes | Cook time: 20 minutes

Ingredients:

- 1 keto pizza crust
- 1/2 cup pizza sauce
- 1 cup shredded mozzarella cheese
- 1/2 cup pepperoni slices

Directions:

1. Preheat the oven to 450°F (230°C). Place the keto pizza crust on a baking sheet.
2. Spread the pizza sauce over the crust, then arrange the pepperoni evenly on the sauce.
3. Sprinkle with the shredded mozzarella cheese.
4. Bake in the preheated oven for 20 minutes or until the crust is golden and the cheese has melted.

Nutritional Information: 630 calories, 40g protein, 8g carbohydrates, 50g fat, 3g fiber, 110mg cholesterol, 1410mg sodium, 300mg potassium.

Made in the USA
Las Vegas, NV
09 September 2023